Clearings

Clearings

Helping Lost Souls Find The Way Home

Maureen Smith

BALBOA.
PRESS
A DIVISION OF HAY HOUSE

Balboa Press books may be ordered through booksellers or by contacting:

Balboa Press
A Division of Hay House
1663 Liberty Drive
Bloomington, IN 47403
www.balboapress.com
1 (877) 407-4847

Because of the dynamic nature of the Internet, any web addresses or links contained in this book may have changed since publication and may no longer be valid. The views expressed in this work are solely those of the author and do not necessarily reflect the views of the publisher, and the publisher hereby disclaims any responsibility for them.

The author of this book does not dispense medical advice or prescribe the use of any technique as a form of treatment for physical, emotional, or medical problems without the advice of a physician, either directly or indirectly. The intent of the author is only to offer information of a general nature to help you in your quest for emotional and spiritual well-being. In the event you use any of the information in this book for yourself, which is your constitutional right, the author and the publisher assume no responsibility for your actions.

Any people depicted in stock imagery provided by Thinkstock are models, and such images are being used for illustrative purposes only. Certain stock imagery © Thinkstock.

Printed in the United States of America.

ISBN: 978-1-4525-9735-5 (sc)
ISBN: 978-1-4525-9737-9 (hc)
ISBN: 978-1-4525-9736-2 (e)

Library of Congress Control Number: 2014908134

Balboa Press rev. date: 07/02/2014

For all the ones who have yet to be found.

Contents

Introduction

I have come to understand that pushing explorations to the edge is what makes life interesting for me. And so it is no surprise that soon after I began studying hypnotherapy, I had myself signed up for a seminar on past life regression and this thing they called spirit release.

Thanks to Brian L. Weiss, M.D., past life regression is a household word these days. Also a wonderful tool for a hypnotherapist to have, and I wanted it. We were going to learn the basics. I soaked them up like a sponge.

Then came the not-so-familiar training in spirit release. As Dorothy Tyo, the director of the Palo Alto School of Hypnotherapy, Palo Alto, California, and instructor for the class, began describing the tell-tale signs indicating one might have a hanger-on from the spirit world, I found myself sliding down in my chair and doing my best to become invisible. Strange and unexpected for someone whose idea of a good time is trying far-out stuff. Typical of someone with an attached entity.

Dorothy had been scanning the room for reactions to her list of indicators and right away zeroed in on my attempt to look very, very small. Hardly there at all. My heart headed straight for my gut when she called my name. I looked around to see if maybe she was talking to someone else. No such luck.

She dropped me into a light trance in her efficient way and we began. The question "Is there anyone there who is not a part of Maureen?" caused the strangest sensation of somebody sliding around inside of me, maybe just under my skin. That somebody was not pleased to be discovered. Dorothy didn't care. She waited for it to respond. And it talked to her! Using my voice. It had its own set of feelings, its own point of view. It's own name: John. The first thing John had to say, "It was an accident!" I had the vague image of a shotgun and a clear impression that our friend John had been playing with a gun when things went wrong. Dorothy gently told him nobody blamed him. She asked him how he liked being inside of me. She got a frustrated, "She won't do what I say!" I had a sudden flash that the back and forth I had going on in my head since I was small was not myself I had been arguing with. It was John. Cranky, pissed-at-the-world John. Dorothy asked him if he would like to have a body of his own again. I felt him imagining the pleasure of having a body under his total control. No argument there. He wanted one! She asked him to look up. I had the sensation of looking up to the ceiling and seeing, with my eyes shut, a blinding light. So bright that it hurt my eyes. Profiled in the light stood a figure with its arms outstretched. John sobbed out, "Father!" I felt him reaching out. Then he and the light were gone.

I felt lighter, clearer. In the coming days, that lightness remained. My passion for my collection of cowboy boots, however, seemed to have vanished. I maintain the possibility that John the cowboy had, in this at least, gotten his way.

So began my new life as a facilitator of lost souls looking to find the way home.

I consider the intensity of the experience of John's release a real gift. I felt his confusion and frustration. I saw the light that opened for him. I witnessed his surprise and relief at recognizing his father. I recognized the burden he had created for me. A heaviness of spirit, and a sensation of carrying some unidentified weight.

I share in this book the discoveries, the insights that have been mine over the more than fifteen years I have done this work. The intention is to offer an expanded understanding of what has been seriously misunderstood. To bring compassion into the picture. And hope for the ones who may be carrying a burden that has nothing to do with who they are.

Part 1: Where Earth And Spirit Meet

An Invitation

Let's say you are told a discarnate entity is siphoning energy from you, or that an extraterrestrial has taken up residence in your energy field, or that the anger and despair isn't coming from you but from a dark being milking your emotions to feed its network, or that you are missing a piece of your heart. Would you believe it?

A surprising number of people have become hosts for unseen beings that burrow into their energy body. Embedded in levels of awareness that are too deep to notice, these intruders drain energy, create interference and confusion, disrupt lives.

Come meet the lost souls I have encountered. Witness with me the unburdening of the humans that have become their hosts.

Peel back the thin layer that separates what we know for sure and the wider world of spirit with me and you may do more than enjoy the ride—you may encounter a way to heal.

The New Plan

When the solution to a problem isn't working, repeating the same solution will not end in a different result.

I am certainly not the first to come to this conclusion—Albert Einstein considered repeating the same thing over and over and expecting different results to be a definition for insanity. It is the reason I was willing to look for another solution to the kinds of unsolved situations my clients brought to me.

Let me lay out this new plan:

First, the unsolved problem may not be coming from the physical world. It could be coming from the world of spirit, in which we all have membership.

(If your eyebrows raise at this notion of membership in the world of spirit, think for a moment of how entranced we are with the rising of the sun, or how our hearts swell with news of a new life, or when the music comes together. The undefinable connection we feel to the ones we love. When for some inexplicable reason, we throw ourselves behind a cause. It is not intellect acting, it is the human exercising the deepest, indestructible part of our being—spirit.)

Secondly, there are other actors in the world of spirit besides ourselves, and some of them may be willing to help. Some of them not. Others may actually be the source of the problem. In this new plan, using our capacity to be in the world of spirit can create the opening to uncover the source of the problem and sign up some new help to set things right.

I want to mention another possibility for the source of a problem: in the world of spirit, there is no barrier to past, present and future. To ourselves as spirit, our entire history, going back for perhaps thousands of years, is as current as today. If, say, you were stabbed in the back in your lifetime in 1560, or you starved to death in 1780, you may be living today with the aftereffects of that trauma. Revisiting the traumatic event in spirit and resolving it is often the answer. Past life regression is the therapeutic term for such an exploration. While this is a part of the work I do, it is not the focus of *Clearings*.

Opening The Link

There is no big mystery to opening the link to the world of spirit. It is only a matter of a shift of focus. We all come into this world with the ability to make that shift, yet it becomes less and less remembered as we move out of childhood. Even if unrecognized, it is there, just under the surface. With a little guidance, it is surprisingly easy to tap into.

Here is how this can be accomplished:

Given the mix of the physical, intellectual, emotional and spiritual in our makeup, if something is off in one area, it will show up in the other areas as well. And so, if we are invited to take a look, more or less, at what is going on inside our bodies and the unsolved problem exists at the spirit level, the problem will also make an appearance in the body. Sometimes noticed as seeing a concentration of color in some part of the body. Sometimes as the flash of an image. Sometimes as a physical sensation.

Then, as simply as asking a question or two of what shows up, the link to spirit is established. It is as if whatever is there uses the connection like a telephone line, sending thoughts through us.

Just as when Dorothy Tyo, my instructor, asked the question "Is there anyone there who is not a part of Maureen?" I began to flash on somebody sliding around inside, just under my skin. So very easily, as more questions were asked of "it," more answers came through me. Both thoughts and feelings that definitely were not mine.

It is these unidentified influences—unknowingly carrying the emotional weight of another being or having another being attempt to get what it desires by using our resources—that are the kinds of things that create the problems which can only be solved when the link to spirit is made.

As the one doing the guiding continues with questioning, the answers keep coming. As thoughts, and sometimes images, popping up in the mind of the person who has been invaded. Going with the principle that if something is not a part of us, it should not be "in" us, the aim is to identify what or who this something is and help it make a new choice. The emphasis here is on choice. At the level of spirit, choice is everything, force is nothing.

Who Else Has Membership

The world of spirit is a terrifically busy place. Most of us see only small glimpses of what is going on around, and, surprisingly often, in us. What follows is a description of what is commonly encountered if there is interference from the world of spirit in the life of a human.

Earthbound Entities

A soul that has been alive in a body, has died and is now floating near the earth is an earthbound entity. It can attach to a living person and draw energy from that person. I have encountered earthbound entities from many categories: human, animal, members of the woodland/nature communities, plants.

An attached earthbound entity is helped to make a new choice and to complete its transition into the Light.

Soul Fragments

A soul fragment, a piece of a person's consciousness, can separate from the whole as the result of a traumatic event. In another instance, it can be a part of oneself that is deliberately planted in another. Another possibility is a shattering of the whole as a consequence of an intense experience that is ecstatically wonderful but contains too much energy for the consciousness to hold.

Soul fragments that have separated as the result of a traumatic event are located and gently helped to rejoin the soul. Soul fragments that have been implanted are guided back to their source. A shattered soul is assisted to gather up all of its pieces and restructure them to wholeness.

Dark Force Entities

A dark force entity is a soul that has never been alive in a body. It lives in the realm of the spirit and mistakenly believes that the Light will destroy it. It is under the control of other, more powerful dark force entities and is given assignments to collect the energies produced from negative emotions. The assignments involve attaching itself to a human, an earthbound, or an organization, and planting and encouraging negative thoughts and feelings to produce the energy it has been assigned to collect. Dark force entities also goad their victims to destructive acts. Some are assigned to interfere with people doing work that will advance the dark force entities' most feared enemy, the Light.

When a dark force entity is encountered, it is removed from the human it is influencing, given guidance to reclaim the Light, and delivered to the Light for rehabilitation. A more compassionate, usually less dramatic and more effective form of exorcism.

Earthbounds And Humans Controlled By Dark Force Entities

Dark force entities will entice earthbounds and humans to make contracts to work on behalf of the dark in return for special powers or to help the earthbounds and humans out of what looks to them like a hopeless situation. The contracts, or pacts, last until the one who has been so entrapped chooses to end the agreement. The dark force entities, who themselves have relinquished their right to choose, expect the contracts or pacts to last indefinitely, thus enslaving the victim for as long as the victim's soul exists.

To put an end to this form of bondage, the earthbound or human is assisted to make a declaration revoking the agreement he or she has made. This act breaks the contract, and the one so entrapped is freed.

Extraterrestrials

Beings from places other than our solar system attach to humans. In some cases they are explorers, scientists. Others are users. Still others are the souls of communities whose homes have been destroyed. All are sent by their controllers to occupy humans.

The invader extraterrestrials—explorers, scientists, users—are reminded of the rights of all sentient beings. Caught in the act of trespassing, they acknowledge their error and withdraw. Those souls whose home planets have been destroyed are given the offer to be taken to their home in the Light. They gratefully accept.

Who Does The Heavy Lifting

As convinced as many of us are that we are alone, nothing could be farther from how things actually work. What might be called specialists in the community of spirit will be right there to help with the ones who have gotten lost and off track and are in need of making that new choice.

Humanity has had a long history of interaction with these beings of spirit: we have referred to them as angels. Believing in their existence isn't needed to benefit from their help. Asking is all it takes.

Angels accompany earthbounds and the souls of extraterrestrials safely into the Light. They cleanse and heal the damage done by the earthbounds to their human hosts. Angels return soul fragments to their rightful owners. Angels encapsulate dark force entities in light, give them their first experience of peace as they are restored to the Light, and deliver them to their place in the Light for rehabilitabion.

The angels' work fits the needs of each spirit in a way that honors the spirit's uniqueness, the godliness of all beings, and every spirit's desire to find the way home.

Making Contact

That part of us referred to as the subconscious is rich with information. There is memory. There are emotions. Decisions we have made about who we are and how we will be in the world. There are links to times, places outside of time. Connections to our soul, and to the souls of others.

All of this richness is available to us through our innate ability to shift our awareness from the active mind, the intellect, to the inner life of our subconscious.

Because we can observe ourselves at this deeper level, we can identify where there are unresolved issues, forms of interference, missing pieces.

This consciousness shift is often referred to as a trance, or hypnotic state. It is no more mysterious than what we do when we begin to relax and then drift into sleep. As a matter of fact, it is the same.

When done with some guidance, it is possible to remain at that level of deeper consciousness that allows for exploration. Not as deep as sleep. Still having an awareness of our surroundings, but with most of our focus on the inner experience.

It is this that forms the basis of the exploration that leads to the discovery of what is unresolved, what is not part of us, and what may be missing in us.

We start with a short visualization to help set up a light trance state. Still very aware of the surroundings with the focus beginning to shift inwards. Then, it is suggested to use, I will say, the "inner eyes," beginning with imagining that there is a special ability to explore inside the body.

Anything noticed—any color, shape, sensation inside or outside the body—then becomes a potential doorway to discovery.

We begin with the question, "If that (for example, tension in the neck or hole in the chest or face hovering over the shoulder) could talk, what would it say?" It could be words, or a sound or a feeling that first comes into the awareness.

I will ask it if it is a part of the client, or if it is something or someone else. Just by being asked to consider that, we all seem to be able to identify what is us and what isn't.

The exploration continues, with more questions to clarify the source. What is discovered can be a memory from earlier in this life, a memory from a past life. It can be an earthbound entity, a fragment of consciousness from another person, a lost part of the self, an extraterrestrial, a dark force entity. The direction of the session takes its cue from this.

It often will take a moment for the mind to accept that this is not something it has made up. As the questions continue and the answers that come become richer in content, some of the skepticism lessens. The mind, still very present, takes the role of observer. It is almost as if there are now two points of focus: an observer and a participant, with the observer part free to ask questions and have them answered without interrupting the flow of the experience.

Whatever is discovered in a session is as unpredictable and unique as each individual. It often happens that the sources of many issues are uncovered.

Now the work begins.

What follows has been taken from transcripts of client sessions. Only the identities of the clients have been changed. The names of the entities are those that the entities chose for themselves.

Part 2: Earthbound Entities

Becoming Earthbound

Let's say, some time in your early years, you pick up the idea of what will happen to you when you die. This idea may come from your family, or the church where you go. Or perhaps as you grow older and begin to make life choices, you formulate your own expectations of what will happen when your body fails. And when it does fail, you may find that things are significantly different from what you expected.

The second most striking of these things is that you've got some choices to make. This "after death" thing is most certainly not automatic.

The first most striking is that you are, well, *you*. You still have the same feelings. You are talking, but nobody seems to be listening. In addition, most people can no longer see you. You still seem to have a sense of having your body, even though (if you're paying attention) you can see that some distance from you is a body that looks very much like yours. And it's not working.

And then you miss the boat. There is a moment when you feel a pull upward, or even notice someone close by who offers to guide you. You choose not to go.

When you make that choice to stay and you have no body to occupy any longer, you become earthbound. This is not a true representation. You aren't really bound to the earth. You are in between. Your being is in a spirit state, yet your perspective—your interests, emotional state—are right where they left off when your body stopped functioning.

Circumstances have radically changed. While things you could easily do when you had a functioning body are no longer available to you, new things are now possible. You can move about easily, even traveling great distances. You no longer tire. Time is all of a piece, it no longer passes for you.

You remain in this state indefinitely, possibly for centuries, unless you are noticed and helped to make the journey you took a pass on when you died.

To the embodied, you have become an earthbound entity. Less politely put, you are now a ghost.

If You Are, How Do You Get Out?

In every instance of an earthbound entity stuck near the earth, whether attached to a person or hanging around in the ether, it is essentially the same process to assist the entity to complete its journey.

First, helping the entity recall those moments before its body failed. Then helping it recognize it no longer has a working body. Leading it gently to the conclusion that it has died. Following this are discussions about how it ended up in its current situation, and who owns the working body it has attached to (not the earthbound). Finally, clearing up the issues that caused the earthbound to miss its opportunity to be drawn up into the Light.

Earthbounds can choose what they do next, just as they were able to choose the fix they have gotten themselves into, stuck between the loss of an earth life and that final transition into the Light. Demanding that they leave can occasionally result in them retreating. It does not mean they won't be back. They must agree to be taken into the Light.

It helps to give them some kind of proof that going is better than staying. This is arranged by having them look up above them. (At this point, the clients who are their hosts often shift their positions, as if they are looking up themselves.) Many times the earthbounds will see first a blue sky, then stars, and finally a light that seems like a sun. They are asked to look into that light. Someone they recognize, often a family member or close friend, will appear.

There is testing now. They are asked to look into the eyes of the one waiting for them, verifying the color of the eyes to be genuine. They are invited to take one finger and touch the hand of the waiting one and report how the hand feels. Sometimes they say, simply, "Good." Sometimes tears run down the face of the client as the earthbound is overwhelmed with the love it experiences.

After this there is no hesitation. The earthbound is invited to say its good-byes to the client. The client completes the release of the bond by forgiving the earthbound. We send the earthbound on its way with a blessing as the Rescue Angels carry it into the Light. The client watches the earthbound go, confirming for both of us that the client is completely free of the attachment.

Unfinished Business

There are earthbounds who stay close to the earth out of confusion and are drawn to people whose lives seem to match theirs in some way. These earthbounds are more aimless, less purposeful, than those earthbounds whose lives have ended in the midst of full engagement in the passions fueling those final events. These aimless ones are looking for more than familiarity. They remain close to the earth searching for a way to finish what they had started. Or for revenge.

Shoo-lup-muh

Shoo-lup-muh, a young African woman, still too young to have started a family of her own, attaches to Sheila when she, too, is seventeen.

Shoo-lup-muh finds Sheila in the midst of feeling isolated and alone and, because of Sheila's vulnerable state, is able to slip in.

When asked what happened to her, Shoo-lup-muh describes to Sheila being captured and taken from her home in Africa during what she calls "the war." She and others from her family are sold to slavers who come with ships. Shoo-lup-muh vividly recalls becoming ill from the stench on the ship.

The slavers, ever vigilant for signs of disquiet among their captives, have a method to send the message that uprising will not be tolerated. They identify the ones among the captives who seem to have some status. Shoo-lup-muh, young and pretty, is a standout. The slavers bind her legs, a weight is wrapped around her waist, and she is dropped into the sea.

I ask Shoo-lup-muh about the better times, before the war comes and destroys her village. She remembers being a loved daughter, not yet promised to another, but very valuable to her people and cherished by the village. She attaches to Sheila in hopes of reclaiming what her life was meant to be, which is, as she tells us, "to be loved and to have children and to share the love and joy of a family."

The two of them are locked in the hopelessness of Shoo-lup-muh's wishes. Her grief weighs on Sheila, even to the point of making it difficult for Sheila to breathe. To end it, I promise Shoo-lup-muh a chance at a new life. I ask her to see what she can see above her.

There, in the Light, are the golden breezes and the grasses and drums of home, with her mother and the women of her village waiting to welcome her.

Before she is taken to them, Shoo-lup-muh thanks Sheila for sharing her body with her and begs Sheila's forgiveness for having burdened her with Shoo-lup-muh's own agony and grief for so many years. As a last good-bye, she tells Sheila, "Stand up straight and breathe freely and love the freedom that you enjoy and cherish the moments of your life, whether alone or with a family."

It is not unusual for attached earthbound entities to be drawn by the similarities they see in the persons they attach to. As in the situation with Shoo-lup-muh and Sheila. Then, the unresolved issues of the earthbound entities are imposed on the hosts in a way that causes the hosts to feel that these issues are actually their own. When the earthbound is released, all that emotional weight is released from the host as well. And so Sheila, with Shoo-lup-muh now gone, has genuinely been freed to stand up straight and breathe freely and love her freedom and cherish the moments of the life that truly belongs only to her.

Xantes

When I first encounter the earthbound, Xantes, attached to Jeff, I find an entity with a personality almost cold in its intensity. Xantes is all about being precise, to the extent that in frustration over my calling this entity Sandy, Xantes lays out the spelling of his name: X-a-n-t-e-s. And a pronunciation, San-theese.

We discover Xantes as Jeff scans his body and notices what appears to be a cone on the top of his head. Jeff sees the cone as a filter, to filter the information coming into him. The filter gives Jeff a name—Xantes.

Once the pronunciation *faux pas* is resolved and Xantes seems to feel I am treating him with due respect, I ask what the purpose of the filter arrangement is. Xantes tells us he has attached in order to be a filter for higher knowledge, so that this knowledge will not reach Jeff.

I have to assume there is no intent to harm, yet this has to have been an enormous challenge for Jeff. I begin the process of releasing Jeff from Xantes' interference by asking Xantes to review what he recalls of his life.

He is a man, living in Thermopylae in the year 11. He is poisoned when he is seen by his contemporaries to know "too much about life, about the future." The poison destroys Xantes' body. He is left near the earth, wandering, out of time and no longer limited by space.

Xantes turns down my offer of a new body and a new life to continue his explorations. He is not interested in taking the risk of becoming a target again. Xantes has found a comfortable place for himself, and a purpose: Xantes will be a protector for the uncertain eight-year-old Jeff who, when he comes to me, is now grown and looking for help because he feels blocked, and not at all protected.

I acknowledge Xantes' honorable intentions. I ask him to acknowledge that, in every body, there can be but one consciousness. In this instance, not Jeff plus Xantes. He seems to have no trouble accepting this and agrees to complete his long-postponed transition.

Xantes' mother, uncle and son stand waiting for him in the Light.

I wonder if Jeff became the son for Xantes that Xantes lost when he lost his life. If it is so, it is an attraction that costs both Jeff and Xantes. For Jeff, a barrier to learning and for Xantes, a brilliant mind brought down, not by a painful and early death, but by the fear that it could happen again.

Risk is only an enemy when we name it such. It was, after all, risk that brought Xantes his discoveries.

It is always possible that with risk, we can fail. It is always true that we can get up again.

Andy

A young woman is enjoying the company of her boyfriend in Peets Coffee & Tea in San Francisco. It seems there is more of a crowd here than she notices. Andy and three of his friends join her, drawn by his longing to be able to continue enjoying a good cup of coffee. He and the three other earthbounds with him have succumbed to AIDS.

The four of them slip in. For twenty-five years, they "drink" coffee through Carla. We find them during Carla's session and promise them they can have bodies of their own again. Better than waiting on Carla to have another cup. They are happy to go.

In a follow-up review with Carla months afterward, she tells me she had been drinking twenty-four cups of coffee a day, including one just before bed. After our session, her coffee "habit" vanished.

I am not saying it is always the case. It was for Carla: if you find yourself overwhelmed by an attraction to something, it could be more than just you looking for the pleasure you find in it.

Randall

At the end of the work day in Ireland in the 1630s, the pubs near the docks would fill with hard-working men looking for a little drinking and a little dancing. Such exuberant drinking and dancing that the party could spill over and onto the dock.

This is where Randall, with his monkey on his shoulder, is when fire breaks out, spreading to the casks of liquor, and then the dock. The only way out is over the edge. Randall dives off and into the water with the monkey gripping his shoulder.

Randall fails to make it out of the water alive. It could have been the alcohol. Or that he had never learned to swim as well as he had learned to dance.

Randall, overlooking the handicap of being without a body, attaches himself to partner after partner. He is frustrated that they die and leave him. "They don't dance for very long," he says.

Randall does not remember how many times he has attached by the time he finds Connie. She, caught up in the terror and excitement of her first crush and hoping to be invited to her first big dance, is easy to enter.

When I encourage Randall to look up, to where he has not wanted to give up dancing and go, Randall finds himself looking at a pub in the clouds with a party in full swing. He is beyond amazed. It is not just any pub—it's his old hangout, and the young barmaid he danced with is there. When he looks in her eyes, he finds them loving and inviting and playful. He touches her hand. "It feels like coming home."

Before Randall and his monkey (who would like to go as well) are taken into the Light, he tells Connie she should dance more. Dance and have fun. Randall's idea of the best advice in the world. And who can argue with that.

Arnold

The earthbound tells me his given name: Arnold. Only after his first offering of what I may call him: "Scrub." And only after my question, "What name did your parents give you?" I am guessing the nickname is a statement of independence, a movement into the beginnings of a new life.

27

It begins in 1840 when Arnold signs on to a ship, at fifteen. He starts his career on board as a deck hand. And so the name.

The new venture does not last long—he is "taken away by typhoid." He recalls his last days on the ship, weak from vomiting and diarrhea. Scrub separates from his body and watches as his corpse is put over the side. He wanders above the water, hoping something will show up that will give him a second chance.

Scrub sees his opportunity when Erica comes vacationing to the Caribbean. He watches her do what everyone does in the Caribbean—swim in the warm blue waters and drink rum. Scrub knows rum. Better than Erica does. He follows her back to her boat. When the rum sets in, he attaches.

Scrub admits to me that this attempt to keep things going for himself has not gotten him the adventures he was hoping for, and has had a profoundly negative affect on Erica. He causes her, in his words, "to produce circuits of reliving the same emotions, not permitting her the freedom to move forward."

He agrees to be taken into the Light when he looks up and sees his parents and the captain of his ship waiting there for him.

Before he goes, Scrub apologizes for bringing Erica down. He tells her that one of her greatest gifts is her awareness and that she was close to dislodging him on her own. I find this amazing. I have yet to work with someone whose attempts to dislodge an earthbound have been successful.

A couple of things to consider here: if you imbibe past the point of being in control, you are leaving yourself open to influences that can be difficult, if not impossible, to shake. And, as Scrub found out the hard way, holding on to how you want things to be keeps the next good thing from happening.

The Cree

He tells us he is eighteen years old, a member of the Cree Nation. In Greta's session, he shows her his first recollection of his life: floating on a lake in Minnesota. It is in the 1850s—perhaps about the time that the Minnesota Territory became a state. He is in a canoe, paddling through the shelter of wild rice on the lake, fleeing from a skirmish with settlers.

He feels the impact of the bullet hitting his shoulder, the blood running down his arm. He loses his balance, falls from the canoe, sinks to the bottom of the lake. He dies, filled with regret for his failure to chase the settlers off his people's land. Bodiless then, the Cree sits in the woods, hoping to find some way to return to the life he has lost.

Travelers come to the lake and the Cree joins them. As an earthbound, he is typically unaware of the years passing. He passes from one traveler to the next.

I ask the Cree to remember attaching to Greta.

What the Cree recalls are his attempts to transfer his efforts to save himself in those last moments to Greta. Frantic energy, pushing her to be incessantly busy.

When the Cree agrees to look up and into the Light, his young wife—the source of his desire to reclaim what he has lost—stands waiting for him.

His solemn last message to Greta: "Be strong. You are traveling in the right. It has been an honor to travel with you."

Flying Bird

Flying Bird has his attempts to bring an end to grievances between neighboring tribes thwarted when he is killed by conspirators from another tribe. Here is how the story goes:

Things had gotten tense in what is now known as the Sioux Valley. Grievances over land and hunting rights are close to the boiling point. There is a threat of war in the air, although none of the elders are in favor of letting things blow up.

Flying Bird, in his early thirties and close to the age when he will become a tribal leader, is, for now, considered to be in training. He still shows impatience and tends to take matters into his own hands. As he does when he arranges a meeting with the other side, taking a chosen number of tribal leaders with him to negotiate a settlement. Even though it is out of the bounds of protocol—in a society where protocol is the fiber that binds the community together—to attempt to settle an issue without all of the tribal leaders present.

They meet in a tepee on neutral ground. Flying Bird initiates the ritual of smoking the tobacco passed in a pipe, asking in essence that all be open to hearing what each has to say. He looks around the circle and discovers too late that he and his chosen few are outnumbered by the opposing tribe. Flying Bird is defenseless.

The attack comes from behind. Flying Bird is felled by a blow to the head. A harsh way to learn that having all your people present is a critical backup to trusting the enemy.

His body is left. A great dishonor.

From his perspective, Flying Bird's life ends just at the point he should have been coming into his own. This and the fact that his body is not returned to the tribe for proper burial keep him earthbound.

Flying Bird looks to find a way to get back the leadership and power the tribe had promised. He comes upon the infant Grace, weakened by fever and hunger. He sees her as, in his words, "one who appears to have great promise and power." It is easy to attach.

He does not come empty-handed: his shattered confidence comes with him, causing him to send Grace doubts about the right action to take, which she mistakes as her own inner guidance. She constantly judges herself.

Flying Bird is not convinced that, given the way things ended, he could have another body and a new life when I tell him it is so. He agrees to look above, into the Light, without any expectations.

Flying Bird sees the tribal village just as he left it. He sees his parents and sisters. His father steps in front to greet his son, and Flying Bird reads forgiveness and welcome in his eyes.

Before he is taken into the Light, Flying Bird tells Grace: "Move forward in confidence knowing your path is protected in the Light. You need not fear any hesitation on your part. You will be guided back to your true path. I fear that my experience has made you hesitate in planning your future."

Even though it appears that Flying Bird made yet another huge mistake by attaching to Grace, it is not true that he learned nothing by overstaying his time on earth. He saw what we, the embodied, often cannot: the guidance and protection that was there for Grace, counteracting the influence of his presence—as such guidance and protection is there for all of us.

The Mage

John notices "An ugly face. A magician" floating near his head. It appears to have on a pointed hat with a brim and seems to be laughing.

If it had been the twenty-first century, the magician would have been wearing a lab coat in a controlled environment. He would have had access to a large body of work to reference as he conducts his experiments.

But it is the fourteenth century and might as well be another planet. He is a mage, not a chemist. He makes potions, not compounds.

I ask this one with the hat, this mage, about the last time he was in his own body.

He is experimenting with a potions formula. It produces fumes which he discovers, too late, are toxic.

Instead of throwing up his hands and saying "game over," the mage stays close to the earth. He wanders, looking for a place to stay, thinking that somehow he can continue his work.

The mage doesn't find anything satisfactory until he comes upon John. He attaches to John because John seems to be a bright, sweet boy and it's easy to get in.

The mage is surprised when I point out to him that he is draining John's energy and is not welcome. I don't mention the obvious: John has not turned out to be at all interested in science. The mage agrees to be taken into the Light. John watches the "magician" doff his hat and wave it as he goes.

The interference this entity created for John was experienced as a fatigue John could not shake. John told me it was like constantly carrying around a weight. I am reminded again how fascinatingly complex is the relationship between earth and spirit.

Ma-ah-nu

Ma-ah-nu recalls traveling in a small boat on the ocean, coming in sight of the shore of his island, riding the waves, anticipating the welcome he will receive and the celebration at his safe return.

Waves sweep over the boat, throwing Ma-ah-nu into the water. The boat strikes his head.

His body is carried from the surf. Instead of laughter and song, he hears wailing. It is then that Ma-ah-nu understands he has died.

His wife and children, friends and neighbors carry him back to his house. They cry and beg for him to return to them. He knows he cannot. Still Ma-ah-nu tries to stay and watch over them. Even as he realizes it is not what they really need.

When Ma-ah-nu comes upon Janet, he sees someone who has traveled, has seen mountains and the ocean and who also longs for something better. He believes he can, with this one, bring her what he is unable to bring to his family. His efforts are futile. He remains feeling incomplete, still suffering from the loss of his loved ones.

I ask Ma-ah-nu if he would like to be complete and united with his family. I am bargaining with him to encourage him to release his grip on Janet. He is very interested.

When he looks up, he sees his family in the Light. Gathered just as they had been at his return to the beach. His loved woman whose deep, deep black eyes reflect his smile at seeing her. Filled with love. For the first time in a long time, he feels united with another living being. He feels filled with warmth and life and joy when he touches her hand.

Before he is taken into the Light, Ma-ah-nu tells Janet, "I'm sorry that I tried to complete my work on earth by joining you. I am sorry that I only brought negative feelings to you and I realize that my work is over."

Earthbounds do not have access to the healing, restorative energy of the Light as long as they keep their focus turned back to the life they have lost. Even with the best of intentions, Ma-ah-nu, in need of healing himself, could bring nothing to Janet but his own suffering.

Smiley

The entity calls itself "Smiley." It sees itself as a light, glowing, and feels it should be attached to a body. Smiley tells me that it needs to be in a piece of meat to be golden and misses being in a human. It describes the point of attachment as a dry place in Gordon where there isn't a lot of *chi*—the life force energy contained in all living things. "It is a break in his energy and he is not as connected to the earth. I don't allow him to circulate."

I can see that we will be needing to rewind Smiley's tape and get this entity back to what it was before it became glowing and desirous of finding a new piece of meat.

Smiley remembers it all: he is a runner, Vince, age 60 in 1952. He smoked, which compromised his lungs and limited his ability to breathe. He died of a heart attack while out on a run. He remembers being taken to a hospital where attempts to revive him were unsuccessful.

"And after that?" I ask.

Vince felt he wasn't done, and chose, even though aware that he had a significantly changed status, to stay close to the earth.

Smiley/Vince has seen what getting into the piece of meat that does not belong to him has done to Gordon. When I offer, he is interested in a way he can get a piece of his own. I ask him to look up, away from the earth.

In the Light, Vince sees a woman with greenish-brown eyes. She says, "I'll be with you." That is enough for him.

Before he is taken into the Light, he thanks Gordon for letting him hang out. What he owes Gordon is an apology for the damage done. Gordon forgives him, finalizing their separation, and Smiley/Vince is carried into the Light.

Captain Robert Sealingham

The image of a large face with black hair, a black mustache and a three-cornered hat flashes in front of Gloria. The first thing it has to say, "This is mine! Go away!" Possessive. And wrong.

It describes the color of the light in its original place and the memory of wind-swept seas, blue sky. I ask if it treasures this memory. It replies, "Yes. But I never felt I belonged there. It was too beautiful for me."

There seems to be more interest in a conversation than ordinarily happens with an entity and I encourage it to continue. I ask it to recall the last time it was in its body. "Those I thought I could trust betrayed me. They distracted me and struck me from behind. I was left in the sand and I wanted revenge."

I ask its name. "Sindbad. That is what I feel it is." I ask what the ones who betrayed him called him. "They called me Captain." I ask what his mother called him. "Robert." His father's name is Robert as well. The last name is Sealingham. The year is 1689.

We move on to helping Robert accept the fact of his death. I ask him to notice where he last saw his body. He sees it lying on the beach, not working. "It makes me angry!" I ask him if he has died. "I don't want to be dead!"

We move on to when he finds Gloria. She is hiding in a bedroom, crying. "She is sending out signals of wanting to leave and travel and go to places I have been. I could find those who did what they did to me." I ask Robert if this is the first one he has attached to. "I have tried others, but they have not helped me succeed. They grew old and died without helping me." I observe that perhaps this is not such a good plan. "It is the only way I know to resolve this anger and this hatred for them." I ask if it is eating him up. "Yes. I need release from this. But I only know one way. That is to pay them back. I have not been able to find them." I point out that his anger has blinded him and ask if he would like us to help him. "Do you have the power?" I tell him, "If understanding and compassion are power, we have that." "I've never solved my problems with understanding and compassion." I ask him if his problems have been solved. The answer, "No." I tell him this body belongs to Gloria, not him. "I understand, but I still don't understand how to solve my problems without a working body." I offer to help him get a working body again and ask him to look up.

Robert sees the sun shining and the clouds parting. When he looks into the sun, he sees his father and the first love of his life reaching their hands toward him. When encouraged to touch one of their hands, he tells me, "I will touch my father's hand because I trust that he loves me." He touches his father's hand. Never at a loss for words, Robert tells me, "I feel all the anger melting. My father's hand is warm and inviting and accepting and understanding and compassionate."

His last words to Gloria before he is taken into the Light: "I never understood how damaging anger can be and I ask her forgiveness for enveloping her in my cloud of anger and revenge."

As Gloria watches Robert being taken into the Light, she notices that when he goes, he takes his monkey with him. She had seen a monkey-like shape darting around her body at the beginning of the session. She observes that although the monkey was afraid of Robert, it also loved him and wanted to be with him. She tells me, "It was the only love Robert knew."

You can let anger fuel your life. If you do, it will blind you and steal joy and peace and happiness from you. That is the price you will inevitably pay.

From Out Of The Water

The victims of drowning who remain earthbound miss a critical piece of information: no breathing means no more live body. Being engulfed in water is their last clear memory. After that, it is as if nothing quite makes sense. The struggling is gone. That stopped when they left their lifeless bodies. And yet, the sense of being who they are has not. They may drift, confused, for many years. Or they may be drawn to the light and energy of humans with bodies that still function. When that occurs, they often attach in an attempt to recover the abilities they lost when their bodies failed. Now, frozen in their own time yet attempting to live through their hosts, they interfere with the lives of the people who unwittingly harbor them.

It does not always happen that earthbounds who drown stay near the water. It does occur often enough to make me want to whisper to no one in particular when I'm at the beach, "If no one answers you, if people are treating you like you are invisible, you may have drowned. Look way up and see if someone is waiting for you in the Light." A course correction for lost souls who otherwise may spend centuries wondering what has happened to them.

Bernard

The largest, most elegant houses in Amsterdam sit on the innermost canals. Bernard lives in one. With his nanny. Bernard remembers having shoes with shiny metal clasps and stockings and trousers. He remembers that the nanny does not seem to care about him (although seeming to be concerned about keeping his shoes and clothing in good order) and he remembers feeling very sad and alone.

We discover Bernard attached to William. William is Dutch himself, recently emigrated to America. I am curious if he picked up this little earthbound back in the Netherlands. It is beside the point. What is needed is to help Bernard get to where he belongs—in the Light.

When I ask Bernard where he saw his body last, he remembers finding himself in the water with a body that will no longer move. He has forgotten how he ended up there. Bernard is also missing that if your body is submerged and you cannot get it to move, you are no longer alive.

In a city built on canals as Amsterdam is, there are many possible scenarios that could end with Bernard drowning. I help him with completing the picture, the accident that caused him to slip and fall into the water, and, not knowing how to swim, to drown.

We have a lonely little earthbound here, now aware of how very lost he is and ready to be taken home. I ask Bernard, "Would you like that, to be taken home?" I ask him to look up. He sees Natalie, his playmate, in the Light, and tells us how much he has missed her. Bernard gives us the okay to ask the Rescue Angels to help him reach her. He goes easily into the Light.

William, unaware that his own feelings of sadness and loneliness could have been exaggerated by something other than himself, tells me he begins to experience what he calls a subtle opening up. Now freed of Bernard's oppressive influence, life will undoubtedly be wonderfully different for him.

Kevin

Kevin finds Sandra at the scene of a car accident. She is trapped in the car, injured and unable to move. My first thought is that this earthbound sees himself as a rescuer drawn by Sandra's distress. Kevin tells us differently—it reminds him of how he felt in the water. He is hoping to experience what it would be like to get a body unstuck and then maybe he could do the same for himself.

It is looking like there are some blanks we need to fill in if we are going to get this confused earthbound disentangled from Sandra. I ask Kevin what he remembers about that time, just before he was in the water. As he talks it is as if he is replaying a video:

He sees a can of soda and a styrofoam cup on the beach in the sand. It is night time. He recalls running, waves crashing. He was having a good time, but the water got dangerous. He had a board, a Bully Board (a lightweight, high tech surfboard). He sees rocks, waves crashing, and he loses the board. He can't fight the water, can't get out. "I can't move! I can't get up!"

Gently, I nudge Kevin to see why it is that he cannot get his body to respond, that he lost his life that night in the surf.

I suspect that now that he is attached to Sandra, those final moments in the water, believing he could not move, are being replayed in her. I ask Kevin how he affects her. "I am making it so she doesn't like to move too much."

In a way, this is helpful. We know what needs to be fixed, and I see the way to do it.

I ask Kevin if he would be interested in having a body of his own again so he can move about freely. Then I tell him to look up.

I expect there will be, as always, a loved one waiting for him there in the Light. Kevin sees a waterfall of light, and, in it, a mermaid. Her eyes are brown and she invites him to come into the water with her. Her hand feels "really good" when he touches it. He will accept her invitation to swim in the Light.

Before he is taken to the Light, Kevin tells Sandra he is sorry he was stuck onto her. She accepts his apology. Kevin goes off to be with his mermaid in the Light. Sandra finds herself relieved of the lethargy she has felt since the accident.

If a soul as completely disoriented and confused as Kevin can be led out of the darkness just by being willing to accept help, why should we not expect that there will be help when we need it—not as we might envision, but always in the way that perfectly fits our needs and our perspective.

Joe

A voice calls out "Help!" and it is not my client, Fran. Someone who recalls having a body. This one saw four-year-old Fran floating on a lake in an inner tube. It watched Fran's inner tube tangle in some bushes, tilting Fran under the water.

Its last memory of being in a body was "in water." The year was 1956. I ask what the body is like. A middle-aged man. He thinks his name might be Joe.

Joe, an earthbound still there in the lake where he had drowned twenty plus years earlier. I ask Joe to go back to when he first found himself in the lake. I ask him what else he sees. A boat. He is unsure of how he ended up in the water. Then he remembers being tangled in something "thick." Joe flashes on another fragment of his fractured memory: he thinks he might have been pushed overboard.

His own memories are jumbled, yet Joe clearly sees what the consequences of that stuck inner tube are to Fran. He tells us he went to help her so she would not drown. The inner tube becomes free of the bushes and rights itself.

Wanting to be helpful, and still a lost soul. Joe was not only attracted to Fran's similar circumstance, he attached to her. He remains attached to Fran, no longer a fragile little girl. She is in her twenties and fully capable of managing for herself. She has felt the drain as Joe draws on her energy. Which is what brought her to me for help.

I step Joe through the process of comprehending that his life ended in the water when he stopped breathing. Time stopped passing for him. Fran and her inner tube entered the water years after his drowning, yet to Joe it was as if it were the day he drowned. With this new information, Joe releases his hold on Fran and is free to be taken into the Light.

I am left wondering: Could a four-year-old fight her way clear and save herself in these circumstances? Would an earthbound have the ability to move that inner tube? I am itching to draw a conclusion from this. I choose to leave the door open and bow to our lesser knowledge of life in other dimensions.

Steven

The entity, first seen by Irene as a blue spot, begins its dialogue with a sharp "Speak up!"

I usually give little credence to commands and comments directed at me by an entity. Calling me a witch, telling me I am haunted, shouting that I should go away, am stupid to look there, does not go very far in getting to the heart of the matter. So, while it might be interesting to know who it is telling to speak up—Irene or me or someone from its past—I let it go and take advantage of the entity's willingness to talk. I ask when it joined Irene.

It was when she was a child and was scared and alone. It says it kept her safe from being hurt. I know better than to accept that as a fact. Whatever it attempted to do to keep Irene safe was getting in the way of Irene making her own choices free of its interference. It has to go.

I switch the discussion to focus on who this earthbound is, how it attached, and what will convince it to release Irene.

The earthbound recalls being a man, aged 19 in the 1940s. He wears forties-style clothes and a hat. His name, Steven. He had been watching Irene when she was in the water.

Steven appears to be pretty darned overdressed for someone watching a girl swimming. If things go the way they often do with drowning victims, there is a good chance that Steven was dressed to the nines when he fell in the water and drowned fully clothed. I ask what Steven last remembers of being in his own body.

He recalls the sky being gray, rain, a bridge and a railing that gives way. That is all. There is no memory of how he went from leaning on the bridge rail to watching Irene.

I see the water as the link. I help Steven recover the missing pieces in his story—the fact of his fall from the bridge into the water and his death. Finally, the realization that the body he currently occupies is not his own.

Not all earthbounds want to have a body of their own again. Steven died young, still enjoying life. With the promise of another chance at that, he lets go of Irene, heading into the Light with the Rescue Angels.

Before he is taken into the Light, Steven tells Irene, "You are a whole person." Yes, she is.

The Good Man

Leslie hears a crunching, snapping sound as we begin her session. This is not an echo from a past life. It is an earthbound that has been with her since childhood, recalling the last sounds it hears. I offer to listen to its story:

It is prehistoric times, a clear, sunny day. He is a man floating on the waters of a lake, the sun warming him, the water calm. He is pulled under. He vividly remembers the crunching, snapping sounds as his body is devoured.

His last thoughts are of regret for leaving behind his loved woman and their children without his protection.

We assist this sweet soul to recognize that he need not be trapped here, bodiless, on the earth. He believes us only when he sees his beloved mate waiting for him in the Light.

There is a piece of business to finish before he is freed. I ask him what effect he has had on Leslie. He has been sending her the thought, "Don't go out in the world." Wanting to keep her safe, as he could not do for his family.

Understanding the source of this misplaced message releases the power it has had over Leslie. She is not in a world with prehistoric, man-eating fish. She is in her own world, free now to navigate it as she chooses.

James

James, the earthbound, announces his presence with a raucous blast from a megaphone. One with yellow and brown stripes. I expect the megaphone to play some role in the events of James' last hours. It is not at all the way his story goes.

James was swimming in a lake in Wisconsin. For reasons unknown, he sinks, gets tangled in the weeds and mud, is no longer able to breathe. Everything becomes still for him.

If there were to be a classic description of the experience of drowning, this would be it. I assume that for those who manage to comprehend they have expired, it is a quick trip from there into the Light. I have only encountered the confused souls who have attached to living, breathing people—souls that seem to have no comprehension of their separation from a body. James, who was forty when he went for that swim and likely overtaxed his heart, is among the confused.

I see that breathing remains foremost on James' mind when he attaches to Lia. He tells us he has caused her to experience "an inability to breathe deep the wonderful pleasures of life and fear things will not turn out right."

Is James stealing Lia's ability to be happy? The sooner Lia has James' weight removed the better. I tell James he has loved ones waiting for him in the Light, hoping those pleasures he speaks of have to do with someone he treasured. He looks up and sees his wife and two children reaching out to him from the Light. They have a great deal more appeal to James than his current situation has. He says a good-bye to Lia and the Rescue Angels deliver him to his family. In the Light, where he belongs.

Omar

I have saved the most colorful drowned earthbound for last. He announces his presence like a man making an entry in a crowded room: "I'm Omar." Spelled out for me, "O-m-a-r." He tells a story worthy of its own technicolor, action-packed adventure film.

He is twenty-two, a hand on a sailing ship in the fifteen hundreds. Says his job is "to move things around and be told what to do."

His last day on the ship, he recalls kegs filled with gunpowder, men running around, ropes, shouting and cursing, being told to move things around in the hold. Then, the ship blowing up and slowly sinking. Omar falls into the water. He is not saved.

Omar talks about coming up partway. "Then I reached down and went into a black man, a primitive." This seems to be Omar's description of changing his mind about completing his journey into the Light. Instead, he attaches to the first available human.

Omar's "primitive" ends up being killed by arrows, or spears. Omar tells us he is unfamiliar with the weapons. Is this another indication that Omar grabbed the first body he could find, not having the luxury of choosing a human with a history similar to his? Then the primitive, Omar says, "went where he was supposed to go." Omar has to quickly find someone else to go into and rushes into a member of the group that killed his host.

Many years later, Omar finds Josh, whom he finds to be very satisfactory. Omar expects that Josh will have "a pretty long life." In addition, while Josh goes what Omar calls "up and down," Omar gets to stay firmly centered. "He had been solid strong before. I haven't let him be the strong one. What I like about him is that I'm just there, right in the center and in charge. I like it here." I point out to Omar the flaw in this system: he is only along for the ride. It is Josh who decides what will happen, not Omar.

This is not lost on Omar. The real reason he stays with Josh is because Omar is afraid he will have to go back to "meet his Maker" as he puts it, own up to what he has done in his life and be chastised (Omar's word) and sent to Hell (also Omar's word).

Ah, yes. The "h" word. I tell Omar there is only understanding and compassion for him, and those who have been waiting for him, in the Light. I invite him to check and see what is waiting for him without leaving where he is now in Josh.

Omar sees a yellow-white light and in it the beatific face of Jesus. The eyes of Jesus are brown and radiant. Omar touches the hand of Jesus: "clean, white, light, pure." I ask Omar if there is judgement in those eyes. Omar tells us he sees compassion and acceptance. He weeps.

Before Omar is taken into the Light by the Rescue Angels, he tells Josh, "You can be the center of your life now." Solid strong, and free.

The Warriors

For earthbound warriors, their battle may be over, yet their connection to that ended life remains unsevered. They stay, even though their comrades complete the journey into the Light. Some because they do not see that their work is done, some from guilt, some from disillusionment.

"J"

When she scans her body, Donna sees a sword piercing her heart. Long and rotating, she says, like her rotisserie. I want to know more about this so-called sword. I ask it to speak. It cries, "Be a martyr!"

I probe to find the source of this voice. It has had its own life, not a part of Donna. It has memories of blue skies and bright sunlight.

Before I let myself jump to any conclusions about blue sky and bright light being signs of a cheerful soul, I ask this earthbound to tell us more.

It is a young man last alive in the fourteen hundreds. The best he can remember of his name is the first letter: J.

"We are fighting for the King and the Holy Land and the Pope." In Middle Europe. J is pierced in the chest with a spear. He falls to the ground, dying on the battlefield under a bright, sun-filled sky.

J is not ready to abandon his allegiance to the cause. Like all earthbounds, he is unaware of time passing. He waits, looking to find a way to take up the fight again.

J describes when he finds Donna. "She asked to be part of the Catholic Church, to be a saint, and she continued into her Confirmation. Her understanding was to be a soldier of Christ and be a martyr." The romantic notion of a twelve-year-old girl lining up nicely with a fervent crusader's dedication to never laying down his sword.

I wonder what life has been like for Donna, with a crusader bent on martyrdom invading her heart. It is past time to set matters straight.

I have a discussion with J. He does not quibble that Donna, and not himself, is the owner of her body. He would like one of his own again. Like the soldier he is, he follows my orders and looks up.

There in the Light, J sees the men that he has trained with and been beside on the battlefield. The friend lost on that final day reaches out for him. His blue eyes feel loving and full of life. J touches his outstretched hand. "It is like we are one person." J is almost home.

Before he goes, J has some last words for Donna: "This idea of being a martyr is way overrated. It is better to live for yourself and not pay attention to the requirements of the Church. And life is better than death and I'm sorry for the damage that I have done."

I ask about that damage. "I have kept her heart heavy and made her feel guilty when she made decisions for herself rather than choosing for the needs of others."

There it is, right from the mouth of a martyr. Choose life and feel great about it. Choosing to live for someone else is choosing death, slower than outright martyrdom, yes, but with the same result. Is this point of view outrageously self-centered? An ugly thing to be called. Only if we overlook the structure of the human heart. When we live embracing and nurturing our own gift of life, we will embrace and nurture all other lives. It is simply our nature.

Andrew

Andrew is a knight coming right out of the pages of stories of chivalry and king and country. When we discover this earthbound, he is attached to Ann, and caught up in the trauma.

Andrew is mounted and in full regalia. It is his first engagement, fighting the Scots for England. He remembers seeing flags flying. It must be before the battle starts, the two armies facing and sizing each other up.

He is unprepared for the gore when the armies clash. He tells us, "It is the blood of many." In the midst of the fight, Andrew falls from his horse. He takes a wound in the side, hasn't the strength to get off the ground. Andrew dies there. "I did not expect to die like this."

I ask what it was that he expected that did not happen. "It was supposed to be like a game, like the games they played in court, but this time it was real." I ask him where he had played these games. In the court in Canterbury, in 1423. A far cry, I am sure, from the no-holds-barred warring of battle-hardened Scots.

I look for a way to help Andrew move beyond those last terrible moments. Easing him back to memories of his family, I ask him about them. Andrew has a brother who fought in the battle and survived. And there are two girls. And a brother who died in prison. Andrew must have stayed close to the family and followed their lives. Clearly more interested in his brothers than he was in the girls.

We have begun to build the bridge that will allow Andrew to release his hold on Ann and be returned to his family. I make the offer. Would he like to be with them again? I encourage Andrew to look up. Someone will be waiting for him in the Light.

It is the brother he fought with. Andrew looks into his brother's eyes and says, "It feels like we are one person, like we are joined as one."

Now there is work to be done for Ann. I had asked Andrew at the beginning of the session what had drawn him to Ann—to establish for both Andrew and Ann that they are two separate beings. She, owning the body, he not. He told us it was her feeling of wanting to escape her life. Then I asked Andrew what influence he has had on Ann. Andrew had caused her to expect that things could not get better, fueling an underlying feeling of anxiety. With

Andrew now connected to his brother and untangled from Ann, this influence ceases. She will no longer dread the future.

There is always a transformation for an earthbound when it makes the connection with the Light. It is almost as if there is a shaking off of the dense emotions that have tied it to the earth. For Andrew, the joy he must have shared with his family in Canterbury returns. Before he is taken into the Light, he asks Ann to forgive him for keeping alive in her the feeling that death is imminent. "Now I see there is life ahead for me and my family." Just as there is for Ann.

Captain Lloyd

Gina sees the form of a man wearing a red coat. She tells me it looks to her to be a Revolutionary War costume and the man in it is insistent. He demands to be recognized. He bellows, "I was to have won the war!"

I ask the earthbound, most likely a soldier lost in some long ago battle, when he came upon Gina, and how he managed to attach to her. He is more than willing to oblige:

"She was physically exhausted, as she was trying to climb a mountain path with her father and their dogs. She was in the area that I was dominating."

An interesting bit of information. This earthbound sees itself as having rights over a stretch of land. I ask our soldier what drew him to Gina. "That she had the strength to persist in spite of her fatigue. She has a lot of vitality." It could be the earthbound recognizes that its own vitality is gone and is hoping to borrow Gina's. Or is it looking for a fit recruit?

"I am angry and dissatisfied with everything that happened. Not what I want. Nothing goes right."

I ask the earthbound entity to take us back, to before nothing goes right. "I am on the hill. I am commanding the troops and have great confidence. The troops are following me. We know we are in the right and these puny farmers are disorganized and hardly worthy of being called a military troop."

Puny farmers. I ask his name. "A Captain. Mark Lloyd." This explains the arrogance. Captain Lloyd is used to being respected, and in charge. I ask the Captain what year it is for him. 1774. The area he dominates: in New England. I'm interested in hearing more of his story and Captain Lloyd is more than willing to share.

"My men are being defeated and they are dying in front of me. I'm angry that they are not prevailing in this skirmish, so I rush ahead with my bayonet. Some dirty, squalid farmer attacks me. He knocks the gun out of my hand and hits me on the head and knocks me to the ground. Then he takes his ax and crushes the side of my skull. He wins and I lose."

It appears Captain Lloyd sees it more significant to have lost to the farmer than to have had his skull crushed. I ask him to check and see if his body works. He admits that it does not.

I ask him to recall finding Gina, moving him forward in time, closer to the present.

"She is walking with one who lives in these parts and she shares that anger at trying to accomplish something that is a little beyond her and I recognize that this anger is a power that may be useful for me to get revenge on these squalid people."

Captain Lloyd is indeed looking for a new recruit. He may have just acknowledged his loss of a working body, yet he is not about to give up the fight. I look for a way to help him accept the reality of his death and the time that has passed since that last skirmish.

"Do you notice squalid people around any longer?"

"They seem to have changed from those engaged in the battle."

"How have they changed?"

"They are cleaner and more organized. There is more structure to their civilization."

"What year was it for Gina when you found her?"

"1991."

I pause as Captain Lloyd does the math. "It appears your plan for revenge has not been successful."

"It's two hundred years, a wasted two hundred years with no success!"

When asked if he would like to have a body of his own again, not necessarily so he can wreak revenge, he states, "I feel so defeated." Still, he accepts my offer of help.

After Captain Lloyd agrees that the body he currently occupies belongs only to Gina and that he will be releasing her body, he asks, "What will I do then?"

"We are going to help you with that. Look up, above yourself."

"I see members of my troop and the General above me!"

"What is his name?"

"Samuel."

I encourage Captain Lloyd to look into Samuel's eyes. "He is approving of me and is pleased with my performance and my work and is welcoming to me in spite of the loss. He seems to regard the loss as a very minor event. He has work for us, for me."

The Captain touches Samuel's hand. "It feels warm and caring and forgiving and banishes any self-doubt or defeat that I had formerly. And he helps me to recognize that those that I despised are worthy of love. He seems to have a sense of humor about my need to hold on to that anger and that revenge. He is willing to accept that part of me."

"Do you need to hold on to the anger and revenge?"

"No. But it is what I thought was keeping me alive. It is difficult to believe that if I release the anger and desire for revenge that I will have any vitality."

Captain Lloyd is unlikely to believe anything I have to say on the subject. I turn to Samuel for help. "Captain, look at Samuel. Does it look as though he has vitality?"

"Yes."

"Perhaps your assumption that the anger and revenge were the only things that could keep you alive is not really how it is."

"Yes. I can feel those emotions melting away and I am coming more in tune with the soldiers that I led, for they all seem to share a lightness and joy which I did not believe exists, and I feel a union with them that I never felt before."

Before he is taken to them, the Captain tells Gina, "I feel that I have made a grievous error to have attached to you in such a violent and negative frame of mind. From this level I can see that violence and negativity are not a true part of life, not a necessary part of life for vitality, and I pray that you can forgive me."

It may be enlightening to ask Captain Lloyd if he means that aggression is not the stuff of life. It is more his issue to work out than it is Gina's and I let it go. Gina forgives him, glad to be free of his burden. The Rescue Angels carry Captain Lloyd to the soldiers waiting for him there in the Light.

Lieutenant Roberts

There is deep sadness in the words the earthbound attached to Helen speaks. It sees its light as once beautiful, but now dark. I ask how this happened. "I was separated from my family in the war and was made to commit many murders. Unforgivable acts."

If this earthbound had come to terms with the residue of guilt he carries, he would not be stuck between the earth and the Light. This will have to be our starting point to free him. I ask the earthbound who made him commit the murders: the commanding officers of the army.

So we have an earthbound who had been pressed into service attached to Helen. His name, Lieutenant Roberts. The year, 1860. He was born in the United States in Illinois. He recalls fighting the Confederates whom he regards as "other countrymen." I am beginning to understand: Lieutenant Roberts must see his actions in battle as murder.

I ask Lieutenant Roberts to return to the scene of his death. There is blood and fighting and torn flesh. He runs away from the battle, is shot in the back and falls in a pile of other bodies. He lies there on the ground, grateful for it to be over.

A technicality in the rules of war had saved Lieutenant Roberts from the disgrace of desertion—since he ran in the heat of battle, even though it was in the opposite direction of the action, he was not deserting. This seems to remain important to Lieutenant Roberts, as he tells us that while he did not want to participate in the battle, he did not go as far as deserting. Still, there is guilt. He feels shame as he watches his family receive his remains, they believing that he died a hero.

Lieutenant Roberts was torn from his family first by war and now by despair. I ask if he misses them and encourage him to look up above him to see what might be there.

In the Light, he sees his commanding officer opening a door. Beyond the door stands his wife in a clean and bright and sweet-smelling dress, holding their baby in her arms. Her eyes are the clearest blue, full of love and invitation. He tells us that her hand, when he touches it, "feels like coming home and being totally forgiven."

In his good-bye to Helen, the Lieutenant tells her that he would like to apologize for disturbing her sleep and making her feel uneasy, as if some disaster were lurking around the next corner. This, the residue of dread the young earthbound soldier carried out of the battlefield. Now cleared away for them both.

Troy

When she scans her body, Joy sees a churning wave. This is a fragment of memory from the earthbound attached to her. Another death at sea, I expect. I encourage the earthbound to revisit that moment. We find him trapped in the water unable to breathe, watching that churning wave. I ask where: in Pearl Harbor in 1942.

This lost earthbound, from my father's generation, touches me deeply. I dearly wish to help this soldier find his way home. He gives us his name: Troy, age twenty-two, from North Dakota. He probably remembers the crew he served with, yet that was not his interest. What Troy wanted was to go back to his body. He followed it as it was sent home. Troy watched his, or I should say, his body's burial. He decided, as he tells us, not to go under the ground with it. I am thinking that was a very smart move. Instead, he decided to look for a companion. That was not.

He finds Joy spending lonely nights longing for someone. I talk with Troy, helping him with a little course correction so we can put an end to his loneliness and free Joy of the weight she has been carrying. Indeed, Troy admits he has weakened her energy and made her feel incomplete. "But it is I that am incomplete."

I take Troy's story as validation of the importance of ceremony to mark a loved one's passing. I would like to add that it could make a huge difference to ones who have died to send out the thought to them that there is someone waiting for them in the Light. They can always come back for a visit once they have gotten safely and completely home.

Sarge

As the details of the earthbound attached to Felice come to light, we are given a sketch of how the earthbound remembers himself: a man others call Sarge, in 1942. He is a soldier, fighting on an island in the Pacific. He is from New Zealand.

We will be helping another lost soldier find his way home. Beginning with honoring him by inviting him to describe that last battle:

Sarge recalls going up a hill. There is heavy gunfire. He sends his troops up that hill. No one survives. He is the last to go (almost willingly), shot in the chest. His final moments are filled with guilt and regret that the men, under his orders, lost their lives. He dies, there on the hill with his men.

It often happens that earthbounds, in that first experience of being released from their body, are shocked by the realization that they have died. It is difficult for them to fully comprehend that they are no longer attached to their bodies. A critical awareness if they are to be effective in completing the transition into their new state. I ask Sarge where his body is, to help him with that reorientation. He tells me, "We did not return home. We stayed on the island, as we could not be identified."

Sacred to all fighting men is the return of their fallen comrades to a final resting place on home soil. It grieves Sarge that this will be denied the men he was charged to lead. He is reluctant to do what he sees as abandoning them:

"I wanted to go back home. I wanted to see my family, and I wanted to apologize to the families of those men I commanded to their death. I could not leave that area. I wanted to go back home."

I am guessing that Sarge used the new abilities he acquired when he shed his body. Merely wishing to get back to New Zealand seems to have been enough for him to transport himself there. We discover this when I ask him how he found Felice.

"I was able to join Felice. She was touring New Zealand. I was hoping to make it back to my family. But I could not find them and kept searching." I ask if Felice was from his home, wondering if that is what attracted him to her. "She was near. She was traveling. I have not succeeded in anything! I have not found my family, nor have I been able to ask forgiveness from the families of the men that I commanded."

Will helping Sarge to understand that, in addition to this slick new ability to travel anywhere he chooses with just a thought, he is now removed from the effects of time passing? I doubt it. It might be more unnerving for him to discover that the people he is searching for may be dead by now.

Instead, I ask him if he would like to find the ones he desperately searches for. "Yes!"

I tell him to look above him and tell me what he sees. "They are all there with their families!"

All that is needed now is to connect Sarge to them. I tell Sarge that one of them is going to come forward from the group. As he watches, his wife steps forward. He describes her eyes: "They are a brilliant blue, so loving!" He touches her hand. "There is such a feeling of relief and love! Such a heavy burden has been lifted!"

Before he is taken to the Light, Sarge tells Felice, "She is free to lift from her shoulders the burden of responsibility for all the things she thinks she has failed at. These are not real. Only love is real."

More than that has been lifted. Sarge's presence had had a tremendous influence over Felice. He had imposed a feeling of lack. As he expressed it, a belief that "There are very few gifts in the universe and it is dangerous to let go of anything. You have to hold it in."

This had been going on since Sarge found Felice when, at thirteen, she was on a plane flying away from home, alone and missing her mother. Felice needs to know how this deadening view of the world played out in Sarge's effect on her. His explanation: "I have not let her get organized and had kept everything piled in drawers and boxes, fearful of any possessions leaving her life, and worrying that these objects from previous years might maintain some essential force from those years." Felice, saved from the devastating effects of life as a hoarder.

Claire

The earthbound attached to Bernice shows her a design in the shape of a chevron. The recall of that design triggers a flood of memories for the earthbound. She is a girl and she remembers her name: Claire. Just four years old. Her home is in France. She knows the year she was last in her body, 1943, and remembers the war and hearing the bombs. And then an explosion.

American soldiers find Claire's body. One of them wraps her in his uniform jacket and they bury her. The chevron design suddenly makes sense to me. Surely, the soldier's jacket bore the emblem.

Claire must have felt safe with them, because she followed the soldiers when they returned home. She tells us she joined their family. Only the family grew and changed, and Claire sought out a new family to join.

Claire comes upon Bernice, struggling with the distress of having her position as the baby of the family usurped when the next child is born.

Claire's own fear and loneliness amplifies the uncertainty Bernice feels about her place in the family. Then this uncertainty is carried out over the years, causing Bernice to doubt that she is loved.

It is clear that no harm was meant, that Claire is truly a lost soul. She quickly embraces the offer to be reunited with her family in the Light. With Claire's passage, the doubt and confusion Bernice has suffered under dissolves.

Spark

Maddie comes to me in hopes of resolving the internal restlessness she cannot seem to calm. Maddie tells me, "I have a frantic energy. It drives me and compels me to hit things." We begin her session with calling to the one who is restless. What Maddie hears is, "Go! Go! Go! Fight!"

As the session begins, the tightness in Maddie's upper chest and a feeling of being stuck signals the presence of an earthbound entity. It is this one, not Maddie, who is so urgently compelled to fight. Its responses bear this explosive energy throughout our encounter. Which begins with answering Maddie's questions about the source of her restlessness.

The entity attached when she was thirteen because "She was weak. She needed something. She had been beaten down." Wanting to help Maddie, to protect her. "I made her strong and made her a great fighter. Wary, almost violent." And very taken with martial arts. When I meet the adult Maddie, she is a martial arts expert.

Good intentions notwithstanding, it does not serve Maddie to have an earthbound entity imposing its unresolved aggression on her. It is time for it to finish what was left undone when its body failed. I take it back to that time and place.

It is in Viet Nam, he is a soldier. I ask him to tell us more. "It's hot. I want to go home." The year: 1969. When asked to recall the last time he was in his own body, he begins with, "It was chaotic. Can't tell what's happening." There is a pause, then, "Shot." His body is dragged. Then flying, feeling "cold" in the airplane. Next, "I'm buried."

I can only guess that death came so suddenly, and in such confusion, he is not sure if he is in his body or out. He is aware of the frigid air of the plane (or is it the lack of warmth in the body, I wonder) as if he has remained in his body, and fails to notice that it is only his remains that are interred. I know that a few questions will clear this up for him. I ask him if he still has a body. He realizes he is no longer in it. This is a step in the right direction.

I ask what happens next. "I'm looking." I want to know for what. He explains he is looking for someone who needs help, and finds Maddie.

If this earthbound is going to be able to separate from Maddie, his focus needs to shift back to his own identity. I ask him to tell us his name. He replies, "Spark." Not his given name, I am sure, but it will do.

I offer Spark the option of having a body of his own again. Yes, he would like that. When I encourage Spark to look up, he is stunned to see his green-eyed sister in the Light. Whatever interest Spark has in Maddie's well-being fades in comparison to what waits for him there. Our Spark is back on track.

Maddie watches as Spark is taken into the Light. When he is gone, she feels the tightness in her chest and the sense of being stuck that had signaled Spark's presence to us at the beginning of her session dissolve.

A Note On Dates And Locations

A less than in-depth search for dates and historical events has shown me that the recall of these earthbounds in terms of events is possible to verify.

Dates given are often close but slightly off the mark, with the exception of J, the crusader recalling last being alive in the 1400s.

The last crusades to the Holy Land were organized by Louis IX of France in 1270 and Prince Edward (later King Edward I) of England in 1271 and 1272. I brought up this apparent discrepency to a friend familiar with the crusades who explained that it was indeed possible for J to be involved in the crusader wars: the crusades to retake Jerusalem and the Holy Lands, begun in 1095, ended in 1291 with the fall of the crusader fortress at Acre; crusader-like actions to take, recover or protect territory from infidels, heretics and pagans, however, continued for several more centuries— and included the expulsion of the Muslims and Jews from Spain in the late 1400s.

There were knights in Canterbury in the early 1400s and while England and Scotland were not engaged in major struggles, there were grievances, especially since the Scots took the side of France in their war with England.

While the American Revolutionary War's full scale battles did not occur until 1775, hostilities did reach the boiling point on April 1, 1774 in Boston. There is a Brigadier General Samuel Birch present in New York in 1783, issuing slaves certificates of freedom for their support of the loyalists.

The Civil War in the United States began on April 12, 1861. In many cases, it was a war of brother against brother.

Japan's attack on Pearl Harbor occurred on December 7, 1941. The beginning of the war in the Pacific that ended in 1945. New Zealand participated as a member of the Allied Forces who fought to take back the Pacific islands Japan had been occupying in 1942.

There were United States soldiers on the ground in France by 1943.

The Viet Nam War was in full swing in 1969.

Hospitals

Souls exiting the planet from hospitals find themselves in the midst of many weak with illness, or purposely rendered unconscious. These souls whose status has so newly and radically changed, out of confusion or a reluctance to let go of life, may look for a way back to the familiar. Attachment is the easy answer for them.

The earthbound entities whose lives ended in hospitals that I have encountered have vivid memories of those last hours. Their deaths are not peaceful separations, looking forward to the future. Their focus is on what is broken, and has ended. It takes very little to help them get back on course and is more a matter of clearing up their confusion about their radically changed status than convincing them that it is time to go.

Veder

Cecilia has a sensation of something leaning on her when she scans her body. We offer it a chance to speak. The first thing that comes to Cecilia is, "I'm hungry."

I continue the conversation. The earthbound entity remembers its name: Veder. I ask how it managed to attach to Cecilia. "She didn't know herself." I wonder about the ways to lose contact with oneself. I'm coming up with a healthy list.

I ask Veder to say more. He is beginning to recall more about his life. He is a family man, he says, and remembers wearing trousers and a shirt. It is 1948. He describes dying in the hospital, feeling very hungry. Veder finds Cecilia there, young and ill. "I take her energy."

I'm guessing Veder was so distracted by his intense hunger, he overlooked the fact that he no longer had a body to feed. We talk more, helping him understand the body is gone, and better things wait for him if he will just look up. It is an easy transition into the Light. Cecilia tells me Veder had one last thing to say to her as the Rescue Angels carried him to the Light: "You are juicy." The "juice" is going to be all for Cecilia from now on.

Theresa

Jackie sees an arrangement of angles in her knees. She describes her legs as looking like they are bent in opposite directions. Her legs look straight to me as she sits comfortably in her chair. I ask the angles what they have to say. "I want out of here!"

If the image of strangely bent legs has not gotten the message across, this certainly has. Someone or some thing is in distress.

When I ask, I am given that it is not Jackie, but someone else. An earthbound entity. A girl, Theresa, and she is seventeen years old. She found Jackie when Jackie was in the hospital for surgery.

Theresa remembers being at a party. She got in a car accident, she says, and died in the hospital. I indulge myself with filling in the blanks. Taking the sketchy description at the beginning of the session and adding in the car accident that brought Theresa to the hospital, I am seeing a broken body. Theresa slips out of her failed body and attaches to Jackie's.

Theresa has told us that she causes Jackie to be in pain. I do not know if Theresa is carrying the residue of her own traumatic death and imposing it on Jackie. What I do know is that there is a way for them both to be released.

I offer Theresa the way out, encouraging her to look far above her. She sees her grandmother waiting for her in the Light. Happy to go, Theresa allows the Rescue Angels to carry her into the Light.

The Cloud

Joanna notices a cloud-like form hovering over her head. It offers the thought, "There's something better."

The cloud tells us it attached to Joanna in the hospital just after she was born, still blind from the birth, lying alone in her infant incubator.

Would an earthbound entity take the form of a cloud? I ask the cloud shape how it affects Joanna, as a way of teasing out its identity. "We have taught her that she is alone and no one will come near her and there is no one to comfort her."

Multiple entities. I ask how many. "Four, and the number changes."

"How does your number change?"

"We have a conduit to draw others here who feel the isolation."

Still unclear about what we are dealing with, I ask the speaker to give us the color of its light. "A billowing blue, very expansive. We now consider the cloud around Joanna to be our home."

"Who are you, the one who speaks and has lost its home?"

"A blue baby."

Finally, something I recognize. I recall the term "blue baby" being used for an infant who appears blue at birth, for lack of oxygen. These infants often do not survive.

I offer this little colony of lost infants to be taken to something better. Back to their billowing blue light. Nothing could please them more.

As a good-bye to Joanna before the Rescue Angels gather them up and carry them off to the Light, they tell her they envy her success at being born.

Scamp

The first thought that comes to Nora: "Break here!" Is this a way of ordering us to stop? I am hoping our speaker is willing to be more talkative. I start with asking if it recalls having a body. It does, and more:

This is a boy, "Scamp," age fourteen in 1978. Scamp was running, falling on the sidewalk, falling in the street and now can't get up. There are screeching tires and flashing lights. He sees his mother crying, running to him and screaming. He is taken to the hospital in an ambulance.

The story is jumbled, ending with Scamp recognizing that he has been hit by a car. He remembers dying in the emergency room. The same one the baby, Nora, is brought to by her mother when she suffers a seizure. Scamp sees Nora there. He notices she is very cold. She seems enticing to Scamp. He tells us he stays around Nora as a companion until she turns eighteen. Which is when she is with a group of friends welcoming spirits in. Scamp accepts the invitation.

Nora had no idea her venture into contact with the other world would be taken as an offer by Scamp. For him, not knowing where else to go, Nora was a safe haven. It will be simple to rectify the situation.

I ask Scamp if he misses his mother, and ask him to look up. Scamp sees "A whole playground with my mother and other children playing. Her eyes are a beautiful blue. She's happy to see me." I invite Scamp to touch his mother's hand. "It feels like the right place to be."

I offer Scamp a chance to give his good-byes before he is taken into the Light. He tells us, "Her spirit is strong and she does not need to seek any other spirits to help her in her life. She needs to play more and enjoy her physical being." Good advice.

I know of no one who would leave their front door open and post a sign reading "Come Right In" over it. That is equivalent to what Nora and her friends did, playing with inviting spirits to contact them. If you do this kind of thing, you are just asking to be used. And you will be. Be smart—don't play with Ouija boards, *séances*, spell casting. The repercussions are real.

The Puzzle

In our preliminary talk, Mona uses images to describe the concerns that brought her for our session. In keeping with her reliance on such descriptions, when she scans her body, it is as if she is viewing a video. There in front of Mona is a white sheep, calmly chewing and staring at her. I will be conversing with a sheep.

I ask the sheep how old Mona was when it joined her. Before she was six months old. It found the way in through the infant Mona's confusion over the messages she was getting from her mother, especially about eating.

I wonder if that is the point of that chewing action. I ask the sheep how its presence has affected Mona. "I give her the message that it is important to eat."

I shift focus and ask the sheep what it remembers about itself. The picture changes.

It recalls being an infant in white diapers in an incubator, wailing and kicking. Not wanting to stay. It is still in the hospital with the other babies when an angel comes to it. The angel comforts it, saying it does not have to stay in its body.

I fail to see the link between the sheep image and an infant earthbound entity. This is of no concern to the earthbound entity, who is more interested in talking about its angel, which it sees with it now.

I ask for a description. "It has eyes that are pink and blue and yellow and swirling. They feel forgiving and loving. It says it is all right to be going back to the drawing board."

I assume this means, in human parlance, that the earthbound entity will be welcomed in the Light. If we are to accomplish that, this little earthbound entity will need to be reoriented to its current condition: attached to Mona.

I ask the earthbound entity to go back to when it finds Mona. "She is in the hospital. There is still the smell of blood and afterbirth around her. I am confused. I know that I have a mission and a plan to be on the earth, but I don't want to stay."

In an attempt to stay, but not stay, the earthbound abandons its body and attaches to Mona. I ask, "Have you died?"

"Yes."

I say softly, "Mona chose to stay, and this body belongs to her. Do you understand?"

"Yes."

"Little one, you can have a body of your own again. Look up. What do you see?"

"All the angels! There is a welcoming party waiting for me! I will be helped to make better plans to be on the earth next time."

Before it is taken into the Light, it tells us, "I'm sorry that I hijacked part of her body in my confusion and I ask that she forgive me."

Mona is willing to forgive this lost soul, finalizing its separation from her. I am concerned that the effects of that hijacking have not been resolved. I ask the earthbound entity to say more about how it hijacked Mona's body and what this has to do with eating for Mona.

"It is a feeling that in order to gain the love of the mother, it is most assuredly by eating that the mother feels satisfied that she is caring for her child, for she is very insecure in her skill as a mother. And so it is that this message is repeated over and over, so that, in some way, Mona can gain her mother's love by eating. It is not an effective strategy."

"Is it a strategy that will cease when you are taken to your place in the Light?"

"Yes."

Mona watches as the little earthbound and the angel are taken together into the Light. I call on the Healing Angels to cleanse Mona from all residue of the confusion and the mixed messages and the false conclusions, establishing the right understanding of the purpose of eating, and filling her with healing, strengthening angelic light.

Jerry

Ray notices a bolt in the left knee. It tells him, "Lift up!" This is an earthbound entity that found Ray in a hospital, feeling weak and anxious and guilty. "I felt I could have another chance with someone with similar emotions. Another chance to be whole."

I know this invasion will not come without a price that will be paid by Ray. I ask the earthbound how it affects Ray. "I make him feel there is something unfinished in all of his life." It gives us a description of how this plays out for Ray from a distinctly other world perspective:

"It makes it difficult for Ray to move ahead. A fragment of himself and his energy spread in all of the issues and problems year by year. Snapping him back like a rubber band to the same issue over and over."

The opposite of the wholeness this earthbound hoped for.

I ask the entity to recall the last time it was in its own body. It recalls an army uniform of khaki-green wool. He is a man, aged twenty-four in 1942. His name is Jerry. He is in France. His knee gives out in pain. He falls down. Others are running past him. Then Jerry feels another pain in his back. "It was not time to go!"

"Who are you fighting for?"

"The U.S.A."

"How is it that you chose to attach to Ray?"

"He is strong, has been fighting and survived, but he is anxious and weak. If I stick with him, I could get home again. Everyone left me. They did take the body home to Kansas, but somehow I stayed here in Europe. How could that be?"

We have uncovered the confusion that has kept Jerry earthbound. In the suddenness of his death, he missed that he separated from his failed body. A few questions should clear matters up for him.

I ask Jerry if he has died. "Yes." I ask him if he would like a body of his own. He does.

I ask Jerry to look up. He sees his brothers, father, mother. His brothers "feel just like how we felt alive and together, working together on the farm in Kansas." I ask Jerry to touch the hand of one of his brothers. The hand feels like "love, home."

Before Jerry is taken home, into the Light, by the Rescue Angels, he tells Ray, "He's lucky to still be alive, and he needs to enjoy his life and forgive the past and release the suffering. What happens in war should not be part of a life. He needs to remove all the energetic bonds that make him recall the events of his military service."

An interesting perspective, this. Jerry is seeing energetic bonds that could be called post-traumatic stress disorder (PTSD). Further, he gives Ray the prescription for removing them. Forgive the past. Releasing the suffering will follow.

Suicide

Suicide victims do not find peace. The emotional wounds that prompted them to end their lives stay with them after death. They enter a sort of grey fog close to the earth, caught up in a web of regret and despair. Often they will seek comfort by attaching to a human made vulnerable by the human's own overwhelming shock and fear.

Jason

This is the case for Jason. He is a young man when he takes his life, recalls wandering until he finds Jessie, fifteen, immersed in the turbulence of her feelings for a despised half brother, frightened by their intensity. She is young, vulnerable in her confusion. It is easy for him to attach.

Jessie experiences Jason's presence as a dark block on her back, pushing her. Our first contact with him is a sound he makes, as Jessie expresses it, "deep down."

I coax Jason to shift his vision away from the dense grey fog he sees surrounding him. It is a big moment for all of us when Jason finally looks up to see his mother waiting for him in the Light.

Jason is the first of my encounters with such lost souls. I find his realization that killing himself has only made things worse for him and his reluctance to trust that he is worthy of forgiveness to be common threads in the perspectives of the ones to follow.

Jessie's story, under her name, continues in the chapter Making Deals With The Devil.

Ralph

There appears to be a gaping hole over Margaret's abdomen. Dark, about the size of a canon ball. Very, very dark. When given a chance to speak, it says, "Come down here with me."

It tells us that Margaret's fear of death had made the attachment possible. Not fear of her own death—the fear of losing the ones she counts on to protect her. I ask the voice what attracted it to her. "That feeling of being overwhelmed and hopeless matched my own, having lost my protectors. Just wanting company."

It remembers having a body, "lying in the mud with gun shots above." This is a young man, aged eighteen. His name, Ralph. The year, 1862. The country, the United States, in the South. He was fighting with his father and his brothers for the South. "We are all lost. I saw them killed and I ran toward the canon shot, not really wanting to survive."

Ralph is in awe of Margaret for finding the will to go on, not surrendering to her sorrow. "For I know that it is wrong to wish yourself dead. Before I died, I knew it was the wrong thing to do."

I ask Ralph if he can forgive himself for throwing himself into the path of the canon fire. He says he cannot. This, then, is the weight that keeps him bodiless and near the earth. He accepts my offer of help.

I begin by helping Ralph to let go of his ties to Margaret, asking if he recognizes that this living body he has attached to is not his to claim. "Yes. It was wrong of me to join her."

I offer Ralph something I notice he longs for and I know is waiting for him in the Light: I ask if he would like to be with his protectors again. He tells me he would like that.

When I encourage him to look up, he sees his father and mother in the Light, smiling and happy. They appear to be dressed in clean clothes, which somehow makes a difference to Ralph. He notices his brothers beside them, happy and healthy. Ralph tells us their eyes are filled with love.

Ralph's father steps forward and touches his hand. "He loves me and forgives me. There is no sin in his eyes when he looks at me. No judgement." I add, "No judgement, just compassion and understanding."

Ralph's last words to Margaret before he is taken into the Light: "I would like her to know that I admire her strength and I ask her forgiveness for tagging along and dragging on her energy."

Solomon

"I am in control of this one's soul energy." A bold statement I suspect is more wishful thinking than truth. Kurt can certainly do without this one's interference.

A few more questions and we know this earthbound entity found the boy, Kurt, weakened by what it calls "a shock." It was attracted by Kurt's courage in the face of it. When the entity attaches, it drains Kurt of the very source of the attraction, binding to him, imposing its own fearfulness on Kurt, pulling Kurt into fear as well.

I take the entity back to its last memories. Its responses have none of the boldness it displayed when it was first discovered.

"I made a grave error. I was very discouraged and fell into a pit of despair. I was not allowed to make up."

Make up for what, I wonder. I am guessing shame dogs this entity and will keep it from saying more. I ask, "Then what happened?"

"I took my own life."

I am wrong. It is not the fear and the shame that has devastated this one, it is despair. I look for a way to offer hope, asking the entity to give us its name as a way of reestablishing its sense of who it was before that grave error. It gives us "Solomon." He recalls being a man of middle age. Then, "I needed to heal this pain."

I miss the logic in Solomon seeing Kurt's courage as a balm for his own despair. When I press him, Solomon admits that his solution is destructive for Kurt, not to mention that it was not his body to occupy. He is willing to go.

Solomon sees his mother waiting to welcome him into the Light. "Healthy, whole, happy." Filled with peace. The balm Solomon could not find. The Rescue Angels take him safely there.

Melissa

Moira describes a rectangle, black, dense, heavy in her solar plexus. It seems to her to be dead. When called on to speak, it tells us, "Heartache. Exhausted, drained so much that it became black and dense and couldn't function or move any more." It claims to be something that has been alive in its own body for some periods.

The vulnerability that allowed it to attach: Moira's experience of an emotional shock. From the entity's view it is like a magician slicing someone in half. It was attracted by this opening, a place it saw it could enter.

Once in, it uses Moira to satisfy the need it sees as necessary to its survival: "An extreme density that I have to maintain, so I suck things in like an energy magnet."

I ask for more information from this strange, deadly thing. The color of the light in its original place, silver or black. It is black in Moira, but it came from silver. It keeps things separated inside of her.

It recalls mental confusion. It was literally out of its body or mind, it is not sure which, in the care facility that Moira had come to for rest and recovery. Its room was on the floor just below Moira's. It had been in the corner of the ceiling for more years than it could remember. It recalls the year 1960, then 1965. Twenty years there in the corner of the ceiling before Moira arrives. Its name, Melissa. She remembers being eighteen.

"Something happened to me. I wanted my body to die. It did. I didn't want to go then. I cut my wrists, or somebody had me cut them. Someone told me I was supposed to. They'd been telling me that for years."

"Are they there now?"

"I don't see them because I think I was able to leave and go in her body."

Gently, I urge Melissa to recognize that she has died and her body no longer works. I tell her the body she is in does not belong to her. "No! I don't want that to be true!"

"Did you notice that it was someone else's body when you came and found the opening?"

"Yeah, but it had this opening. She was frightened and she had huge pains emanating from her. I thought I would fill one of those holes for her."

Bargaining. Claiming to be helpful. I tell Melissa she cannot stay.

"Where would I go if I left?" That is as good as an agreement to leave.

"Would you like to be safe and not frightened?"

"I would. I feel pain where I am now because this body and mind are in pain. Sometimes I wish I hadn't done this."

When I ask her to look way up above her, Melissa sees the sun. I encourage her to look into the sun and tell me what she sees there. "People." I ask if she knows any of them. She does not. I ask her to notice the one who steps forward. "She's in a dress. Her eyes are blue. They feel soothing." When she touches the woman's hand, Melissa finds it feels "kind of warm and there's a light when the two of us touch." Good enough. Melissa may not be able to identify who waits for her in the Light, as most earthbounds do, yet she feels safe with the connection. She will go.

Before the Rescue Angels carry Melissa into the Light, she tells us, "I know that I blocked her, kept her feeling the separation of her head and her lower body. I feel sorry for that." Moira, now relieved of both the blockage and the energy drain Melissa caused, is free to focus her energies on her own healing.

Caroline

The entity seated in Claudia's hip has every intention of staying right where it is, claiming, "There is freedom here." I ask the color of its light. "Blue, same as here." The language of the young. I ask its age: sixteen, and a girl. The name, Caroline. She found her way into Claudia, also a teen, through Claudia's fear.

Caroline keeps her memory of the pain she experienced alive and active in Claudia. If she is to release Claudia, we will need to know the source of what Caroline calls "great pain." I ask her to share her story.

She recalls running down a deserted hall with tile walls in a hospital gown, jumping through a plate glass window. She was cut, and then stopped moving. Caroline relives the regret she felt when she died.

She looked to repair the mistake of killing herself. She chooses Claudia, "Someone with life and who would not be judgmental and would be sympathetic."

I ask Caroline if she would like a new body of her own. She tells me she is worried that she would be punished for ending her life if she were given a new body. With the reassurance that there would be only compassion and no punishment, she looks into the Light.

"I see the ones I was running away from, including my mother and father."

I encourage Caroline to touch her mother's hand. "She has forgiven me. I can forgive myself now and move on." As direct as she was when she was first discovered.

Before Caroline is taken into the Light, she thanks Claudia for her compassion towards her and asks Claudia's forgiveness for having to carry Caroline's burden for those years. Indeed, Claudia is in her fifties.

With that final good-bye, the Rescue Angels lift Caroline out of Claudia and into the Light.

The hardest act for suicide victims is to forgive themselves. If they do, and when they do, they can see the Light waiting to welcome them. No judgement, no punishment, only acceptance. Should we not, even without understanding the devastating choice they have made, offer them that same compassion?

Animal, Vegetable, Mineral

I was astounded to discover entities attached to humans that were distinctly nonhuman, very aware of who and what they were, and just as confused at the end of their days as the deceased people I had encountered clinging to my clients.

I am left to conclude that we are ever so more connected to all beings on our planet than we think. I suppose it should have not come as such a shock. We are, after all, made of the same stuff.

An Animal?

When the entity attached to Bonnie came out with "I'm an animal," I thought to myself, we must have someone feeling guilty about how things ended. Then came the description of what it was doing there, attached to Bonnie. Keeping her warm. A kindness. No guilt there, I thought. I probe to see what it remembers about its life. It was two years old in 1976. Things are not adding up—what two-year-old would have viewed itself in such an incriminating way that it would call itself an animal? I ask what it recalls about being in its body.

It is a wild animal, a civet cat. With fur and a long tail. It died of starvation in its cage. And still it seems to hold no ill will towards humans. If there is guilt to be assigned, I am thinking, it would be to the one who left it to suffer and die.

I do not know how animals make their last journey into the Light. I suspect they need, as humans do, to be aware that their life has ended. The little civet seems to understand now how it is that it is freed from its cage. I ask the Rescue Angels to carry it to the Kingdom of Animals in the Light.

Samantha

The attached entity cries out, "It hurts!" There is some confusion at first, as it claims to be a part of Susan. It does, however, remember that it joined her when she was in her early twenties and in despair, and so certainly separate. I check to see if it recalls its own beginnings. It remembers the light being a deep forest-green. The year, 1781. It's age, 11. The name given is Samantha.

The year, the age, the name given all point to an earthbound entity, most likely a girl. Though that deep forest-green business doesn't fit the pattern of a lost human soul. Humans remember the light at the point of their beginning to be a golden-white. I am wondering what is up, and then Samantha tells me she is a cow. This is a cow! Susan has a cow attached to her!

Our conversation continues. Samantha lost two calves. She seems distressed when she says, "I was trying my best!" and remembers somehow getting tangled in a fence. She understands that she is no longer alive, and happy to be carried off by the Rescue Angels to the Green Pastures of the Light.

Samantha isn't clear about how her life ended. Nor am I. If I were to venture a guess, I would say that dear, dedicated Samantha was done in by that fence. Having known sorrow herself, she is drawn to Susan, who, now in her thirties, is an animal healer by profession. I see the possibility that those abilities in Susan that blossomed into a career were what made Samantha feel so at home with her.

"The Source Of Life And Refreshment"

Ginny feels her throat closing. Someone begs, "Help me breathe again!" This is an earthbound entity that attached when it saw Ginny swimming in the ocean, all decked out with flippers and goggles and what looked like a large hook in her mouth. It watched Ginny swim up to the surface and then go down again, seeming in perfect harmony with her surroundings and managing to breathe, even with that hook stuck there.

This fascination with being able to breathe with a hook in the mouth was not the perspective of a human. A human would be more likely to know about snorkeling.

Since by now I had encountered a couple of animal attachments, I was ready for just about anything. I ask about the light where it's from: blue-green. This is looking oceanic to me. And so I ask.

It is a fish. It recalls its mouth being stretched by a hook, coming out of the water, flopping on the boat. When it saw Ginny seeming to do fine with a hook in her mouth, it thought it could learn to do that as well.

Could it be that a creature who dies in a way not natural to it misses recognizing when it is separated from its body? I decide to explain the fact of its death to the fish. I ask if it would like a new fish body. Oh yes! It looks up into the Light and sees "an abundance of shiny silver fish swimming." A school of fish souls in the Light.

The Rescue Angels carry it gently into the Kingdom of the Sea Creatures in the Light. Before being taken, it says to Ginny, "Love the water. It is the source of life and refreshment."

It was not a carefree Ginny the fish had found while she snorkeled. The fish was first attracted to Ginny by the young woman's feelings of isolation. I am observing a pattern here: are animals attracted to humans who are in the midst of some kind of struggle?

This attachment did not come without a price. I had asked the fish how it has affected Ginny, expecting that there must have been some kind of disturbance in her throat. The fish described that it had been an obstacle to Ginny's swallowing the right foods and searching for the right breath. It had passed its struggle to breathe on the deck of the ship on to Ginny. Translated into human terms, its struggle became Ginny's constant questioning of her own judgment regarding two basic components of survival: eating and breathing. The removal of the attachment has been liberating both for Ginny and a little lost fish.

In The Restaurant

My theory about animals who die in a way not natural to them being confused about what to do once their bodies are gone is given more validation when Alice and I find the fish shape she has noticed to be not a fish but an eel. She picked it up, or, I should say, it latched onto the skin on her arm, in a Vietnamese restaurant.

I ask the eel to recall what had happened to it. Here is how the story goes:

Alice was having dinner out after a movie which had terrified her and left her shaken. The restaurant had a tank of live fish where the eel had been kept. All the eel remembers is being chopped up and feeling confused, apparently unaware that its body did not survive the chopping. Freed of its body, the eel searched frantically around the restaurant for a place to go. Alice was the only one who was not repulsed by it. And so it attached to her skin and had been feeding on her ever since.

I make a note to myself: Alice's unsettled state seemed to be the vulnerability that allowed the attachment to occur.

The eel finds it distasteful being attached to Alice, and Alice is drained by its presence. Both are happy to have the situation rectified. And so the eel is carried off to the Realm of the Sea Creatures in the Light by the Rescue Angels.

The Shadow In The Head

At the beginning of his session, Mark notices a shadow inside his head. He describes it as located behind the pituitary gland. This is a strikingly specific description, especially coming from Mark, who has no medical background beyond the everyday knowledge of a layman.

I ask the shadow to speak. "We like being dense." I ask who it is that likes being dense. It remembers being a bird, a seagull, flying around and then its body got smashed. It has a memory of flying near a pier just before the smashup happens. It tells me, "I left there and had to find some place to go into. It happened so fast! Ah! It was gone and I had to find some place to go into." It's a good guess that the "it" that was gone is the seagull's working body. The bird sees the boy Mark at the pier, as it says, "standing there."

The seagull describes moving in and starting to make a nest in Mark's head. I am thinking this may explain the shadow Mark sees. The gull, still chattering away, says, "A tumor, nothing bad, not cancerous. I was just trying to make a nest. It took a long time to slowly grow, grow and grow. I'm still hanging around in here, and my nest's all gone, there are just a few shreds left. It looks really shitty."

This seems colossally crazy to me. A bird entity, invading the brain and, in an attempt to nest, forming a tumor. Then complaining that its "nest" has been destroyed.

I remind myself that my job is to help free Mark of the interference, no matter how wacky the source may seem.

I ask if it thinks it has done harm to Mark with its nesting. "Yes. But I'm just barely hanging on. I'm still hanging around in here. But my nest's all gone. There's just a shadow of it. I'm hanging out in this little piece that's left. It's all cut out and there are only a few pieces left."

Maybe this is a credible story. The gull seems to have just described how surgery to remove a tumor would likely be performed.

I get back to the work of getting this entity gone. I ask if it would like to have wings again. "Yes!" It would like to have a body with wings again. I ask the gull to look up. "I see a big bird with big wings, a swan." It looks in the swan's eyes, and they feel "peaceful and relaxed, and still powerful." I ask if it would like to be with the swan. "Am I going to take his body?"

First it loses its life by slamming into a pier, then it tries to solve the problem by causing a tumor to form in a boy's head, and now it wants to know if the swan it sees in the Light will be giving over its body. No insult to the species intended, but what a bird brain! Patiently, I explain to the gull that it is just going to be *with* the swan in the Kingdom of the Beings of Flight in the Light, it will not *be* the swan. I ask if it would like that.

"Will I get my own body? Will I get born or something? Go back to an egg and get a whole new life? I could be like the swan's baby or something?" I view this as an improvement over the gull's first idea that it will co-opt the swan's body. We are making progress. I tell it, "I don't know if you would be the swan's baby, but you would be back in the cycle so that you can be a bird again." The gull says enthusiastically, "I would like that a lot!"

Before it is taken, it tells Mark, "I'm sorry for draining you so much. After the operation, there was not much space left and I had to feed on you a lot. I got really scared. I got completely drained trying to survive. We'd both be much happier if I left and had a body again."

Ah. It recalls the operation that removed its "nest." What is more significant for Mark, it acknowledges the harm it has caused and clarifies that the harm will now cease.

Mark finds it hard to forgive the bird. I tell Mark the forgiveness is not an act of kindness for the gull, but necessary for his release from the bird to be complete. The gull apologizes again for feeding on Mark. Reluctantly, Mark forgives it.

With this, the gull's invasion of Mark ends. The Rescue Angels carry it off to the Kingdom of the Beings of Flight in the Light.

Oscar

Liz has the impression of looking out of the eyes of a snake's head. Glistening skin around her. She feels the teeth. Black eyes, alert, ready to pounce. There is a filmy membrane all over her face, her teeth, her tongue. Light-green mottled skin from her lips to over her head. A sensation of leather. A white-beige throat, all the way down to the gut. "My tail is swishing," she says.

How could this be anything other than a snake? It has so completely bonded to Liz that it seems, at the moment at least, to have become her persona.

I invite the snake-like shape to say more. "I'm looking for the enemy. I am in danger, always in danger! I always suspect that something is going to kill me, hurt me, trample me. Trespass on my turf." I want to encourage it to engage with me and ask what it remembers about the light in its original place. "It is reflecting off desert and stone. Gold, but not resplendent gold, dirty gold. I need to find a rock!" It is back to guarding itself. I try asking if it has a name. "Oscar." This is a sure sign that it is willing to talk, just as surely as saying "What is your name, little boy?" will get a child's attention. Only Oscar is no little boy.

I ask Oscar if he is a being that humans would call a snake. He is. And what kind of being he would consider himself? "Desert creature." A desert creature, far from its desert home, is peering out of Liz's eyes.

He discovered Liz when she was a child, finding an entry when she was being punished. Oscar's recall is vivid: "Father spanked her. Took down her pants in front of company and walloped her. She was humiliated, betrayed. She lost confidence in Father. Hated herself. What was wrong with her, she asked. 'Why am I so bad? Not bad, why am I so unacceptable?'"

The attraction: "She was cute and unhappy." Oscar thought he could help by keeping her coiled up inside herself in order to protect her. "No trust of herself!" This might be a great tactic for a snake. It has been far from helpful for Liz.

It is time to help Oscar move along, starting with helping him to reconnect with his own history, the last time he was in his desert-creature body.

"Tortoises, other snakes, coyotes." A coyote ate him. He corrects this with, "Well, I don't know if he ate me. He lacerated me, killed me."

I ask Oscar if he is aware he has died. He is. I ask what happened next. I am expecting the usual tale of wandering about and somehow coming across Liz in the midst of that awful spanking. "I went up to the sky and saw souls of Mexicans."

I go with his story. I ask if he knows these souls. "Yes. They also harassed me when I was alive and they were alive, but they didn't kill me. We recognized and acknowledged each other. And they apologized. They were frightened of me. And I can see I was frightened of them. So much energy wasted! Regrets! Remorse! Mine and theirs. We all go up into the sky together and we dissolve. Atoms float away. All our atoms get mixed up together and we are happy."

Wow. Oscar the snake having a soul encounter. And with his old adversaries. With all forgiven and ending in bliss. Then how did his atoms get reassembled back into his desert-creature self, find Liz and burrow into her?

I make the choice to help Liz first and deal with my curiosity second.

I ask Oscar to skip forward to when he finds Liz. "Poor little girl! The guests are there, embarrassed and upset." Then it is as if Liz, not Oscar, is recalling the event. "They try to restrain my father. He won't stop. (In a soft voice) But she is just a little girl! (In a stern voice) She's gotta learn!"

Oscar curls up inside Liz, gets warm. "I'll stay here a while." I point out to Oscar that it is one body, one consciousness, not one body and two consciousnesses. Usually enough to get the message across: this body belongs to Liz, not Oscar. I get an indignant, "Why?!" Foolishly, I ask him if he would like someone else to be inside him. That would be fine with him. I ask what he would do if that person wanted to do something different from what he wants to do. "Get rid of them!" I say, "Maybe Liz would like to have her body all to herself." Offended, Oscar growls, "Ungrateful! Ungrateful!" This is one argumentative snake.

I tell Oscar what he already knows and is reluctant to admit. This body belongs to Liz. He doesn't seem comfortable and doesn't like being there either. I ask if he would rather have his own beautiful body, a new one just for him. "Yes!"

Tackling the confusion surrounding his return to earth, I tell Oscar that I am not sure how it is that he mixed with other atoms and thus did not complete his transition into his home. Oscar corrects my misperception. "Well, we were in our home." I ask where that was. "In the sky." Then what is he doing back here? He does not seem to know. If Oscar is clueless, there is no point in pursuing it.

And so I offer to clear things up for him so he can continue his life as a beautiful desert creature with his own body. I ask him to use his flashing black eyes to look straight up above him. He sees white light. When asked to look into it, he sees the Mexicans waving at him, smiling. "They say, come play with us." This he would like.

In parting, Oscar says to Liz, "I don't know if I protected you properly. I'm very confused about that. I'm sorry if I hurt you. I didn't mean to hurt you. I meant to help you." Liz forgives Oscar. The Rescue Angels are called on to carry him into the Light. She watches until he is gone.

"We Are Calling For Attention"

An intelligence harbored in the middle of Joyce's brain accepts the invitation I offer it to speak: "We are calling for attention." It identifies itself as a group of multiple earthbound entities. The color in their original place, the place where they were born, is green and blue. They explain that they are not born to my environment. Their description continues with, "We have been alive in the bodies of the men of the forest." They give me one more piece of the puzzle: they are from Borneo.

I am baffled by this and set it aside. I move on to help reconnect them with their last clear memory. They recall wind and rain. Could not breathe. Gunshots, terror, sorrow, falling, grief. The grief and sorrow take them over. This one piece of the puzzle I comprehend. Their sudden and violent death has caused them to lose their way.

Thousands of miles away, Joyce watches a documentary and witnesses their death. Her heart goes out to them. She reaches out her arms to protect them, and they attach.

In stark contrast to the crumbs they have dribbled out to me in identifying themselves, they provide a blazingly clear assessment of what Joyce's attempt to provide them a safe harbor has cost her.

Their presence has made her feel impotent to move ahead because the grief is so paralyzing.

When I offer them the option to be delivered to their true home, there is no quibbling about it being time for them to move on.

I am trusting the Rescue Angels to figure out where that may be when the earthbound entities give me one last set of clues. They are covered with long orange fur. Their arms are long, fingers are brown. Their feet and hands long to grip tree branches. Then they spill the beans. They are orangutans!

Before being taken to the Kingdom of Animals in the Light, they ask Joyce for "The good work you can do for our kind." An enigmatic request, and so like the little I have come to know of them.

I have no doubt that Joyce will figure this one out. It is she who explains to me after her session that the indigenous people of Borneo refer to orangutans as The Men of The Forest.

I am left impressed with the intelligence The Men of The Forest displayed in playing their mind games with me. They must have thought me hopelessly dense.

In retrospect, it saddens me to realize that our limitations in recognizing the treasures hidden in the ones who share, more than occupy, this planet with us are leading to irreparable losses.

I place my hope in Joyce finding a way to shine the light.

Tight, Wound Up And Very, Very Angry

David notices a bulging out area in his chest. When asked to speak, it says it is tight and wound up and angry at being stuck in him. David feels it may be a part of himself. A past life? I urge David to follow the feeling. He tells me it feels like a lion that is caged and wants to lash out. David howls and roars. Even in the face of this compellingly visceral display, my money is on this not being David.

The one who does the howling and roaring has more to say: it doesn't like being stuck in someone else. Then it offers us a description. It is a lion, captured and whipped by circus people. It wants to get out of the cage and rip them apart.

So how does a furiously frustrated lion come to be stuck in David, I wonder. Its answer: it found him when David was three. "He had things to be angry about as well," it tells me.

We are given more of the lion's story. It is frustrated that it has been unable to scratch or kill anyone. It recalls being whipped and wanting to lash out. It finally roared and reached out and clawed the one tormenting it. For this, it was shot and killed. It regrets its death, not getting the satisfaction of seeing if the man with the whip died from his wounds.

And now, thinking that it would have a refuge, and a route to revenge by attaching to David, the lion finds itself caged within him. It is very interested in getting out of David's body. It just doesn't know how to do it.

I ask the lion to look up above it and into the Light. It tells me it sees Aslan, the lion from Narnia, and weeps. I am intrigued by the possibility that this lion was listening in when David read C.S. Lewis' classic. Or could it be sorting through David's memories looking for a way to express what it sees and comes upon Aslan's story?

The Aslan in the Light has eyes that feel big and strong to the lion, like it wants to be. All its frustration and confusion dissolves. Before it is taken to the Light, the lion tells David that he doesn't have to feel angry and trapped and rebellious. "That was me, not you." With our blessing the Rescue Angels carry it safely to the Kingdom of the Magnificent Beasts in the Light.

The Purple Light

The first thing Doris notices is a purple light in the shape of an eggplant in her gut. It is smooth, shiny, and pulses lightly, growing slowly and nudging itself larger. It cries out, "Feed me!"

We establish that it has had a body. It recalls purple light. I am thinking this could go anywhere. I ask it how it got inside Doris.

Her appendectomy. I am aware that these things happen in hospitals and expect we will shortly discover an attached earthbound entity. I invite it to tell its story. It spills out in a rush, as if the entity has been frantic to tell it.

It feels lost and doesn't know who it is. It recalls an angry tigress who wants to eviscerate Doris because Doris is juicy and it's hungry and it wants to eat Doris' guts. It recalls that the last time it had something to eat is weeks ago, maybe longer. Her last meal was a gazelle. She lost her family. She was eating and, when she looked up, her family was gone. She felt alone and abandoned. She went looking for them and killed someone, a human man. Then people came after her, so she started to run and ran out of her territory. She didn't know the food sources in this territory. She ran and ran and became very tired and angry and sad. She saw someone walking in the jungle. She pounced on him and got him by the neck. He got away. She was more hungry and more frantic. She laid down to rest. She was captured in a net and killed.

The long and short of it is the purple eggplant-looking thing is not a human soul at all, but a lost, hungry tigress. By the end of the telling, she seems to recognize what she is or was. We now need to help her get clearer on her current status.

I ask if her tiger body works any more. "It works, but not in the material plane." When I press, she admits that she knows she has died. She misses having a tiger body. Even more, she does not want to be alone. I offer to help her with that.

The tiger looks up into the Light, sees her cubs calling her. Before she is taken into the Light, she apologizes to Doris for hurting her, but says it was her nature to feed herself. "And that's just the way things are." Philosophy from a cat.

The Rescue Angels deliver her to the Kingdom of the Animals in the Light.

Once the Healing Angels finish the work of cleansing and healing Doris from the effects of having a tiger in her gut, she says in relief, "I am light and I am whole!" And so must be our tigress.

Fun

It begins its communication with a wistful, "I wish I were gone." The light in its original place is blue-green. Blue-green like water? I wonder. I ask what year it is for it. "We keep time differently." Not human. I ask about the last time it was in its own body. "I am in the water." Not drowning, just in the water. I go for a name to keep the connection with it going.

Sylvia tells me she is given the sound of a high-pitched screech, too high for her to replicate with her own voice. Perhaps the entity will give us a translation. I ask it to translate the screech into human speech. It obliges us: "Fun." It tells us it is a dolphin. I cannot help but call to mind the little that I know about its species. The friendliness, the willingness to do its best to connect.

Fun attached to the teen-aged Sylvia when Sylvia was in Mexico, feeling isolated on the seashore and wanting to swim, but afraid to go into the water. Fun wanted Sylvia to come in the water with it. And so Fun, true to dolphin form, was looking for a way to help.

As I well know, an attachment provides no benefit, no matter how well-intentioned. The dolphin has caused Sylvia to experience headaches and heaviness. They both need freeing.

I help Fun to reestablish its last hours in a dolphin body. The cause of Fun's death: it had swum into a net, was "pulled from the water with fish—the only one in my family." Fun was crushed when the fish were processed.

Fun asked "to be with my family." I called on the Rescue Angels and they carry Fun to the Kingdom of Sea Creatures in the Light.

Keeping Her Propped Up

A rod, or stick appears in Maggie's lung. "We have had to prop her up." I ask what it is that must prop Maggie up and am told it is not the earthbound entity that I expect, but a plant! I want to know how this happened.

This is Maggie's house plant. It saw her leaning precariously out the window of her apartment. Fearing that Maggie would fall, it attaches to keep her safe.

This is my first plant. I expected it would be my only plant. I ask few questions, wanting to simply make sure Maggie was no longer affected by its stiff presence.

I have to assume that it was alive in its own plant body when it reached out to her. It is separated from that body now and, not knowing if it could be returned to its pot so many years later, I arrange for it to be taken to the Gardens of the Light by the ever accommodating Rescue Angels.

Santa Cruz

What appears as a hole in Vicki's left cheek says, "Open up!" It recalls the light being a bright yellow. Curious for it to be aware of the light being bright, but not for long. It gives me its last recollection of being in a body as when it was "alive in a plant." And so its memory of the light would be a bright sun. I have met my second plant entity.

It well remembers its life as a plant. It recalls the coast in Santa Cruz, California, in an artichoke field. Then being boiled in water when it wanted more than anything else to make a seed. Then it was stuck in a mouth. It does not recall being chewed and swallowed, which had to come next. It must have bailed at that point. Its next memory is of finding Vicki when she was small, walking and feeling, as the artichoke describes, "that she did not have enough to eat."

The artichoke tries to take root in Vicki's mouth, causing her to have dreams of her teeth being uprooted and falling out. What is more, it has affected Vicki by giving her "a feeling of not enough of the right things, not enough to grow."

The logic of why this artichoke entity decides it can reestablish its life as a plant in someone's mouth and move forward with its seed-making plan there escapes me. I certainly get that it has no hope of feeling nourished if it is lodged in Vicki, and seems to have exacerbated those same feelings of malnourishment in her. This is a nightmare for both of them.

I offer the artichoke what it is after: to be able to grow its seeds. When encouraged to look into the Light, it sees drawers and drawers of seeds being cared for by light beings, giving them gentle tending and watering. It tells me it is looking forward to being able to make seeds. The Rescue Angels gather it up and carry it off to the Light.

Cedar

Doreen sees a vertical shape, like a stripe, pressing on her abdomen. The stripe demands, "Let me out! I want to go home!" Good. It should be easy to get whatever is attached to Doreen to go. Human, animal, vegetable, whatever.

First it needs to be aware of how it came to be there in Doreen.

I ask when it found her. "She was lonely and looking for a friend." It felt the girl Doreen's desire to bond with her environment, with the trees and the rabbit in her yard. Animal, vegetable. I do not even try to guess.

I ask about the last time it was in its own body. "I am a green tree, an evergreen tree. I don't understand how humans take in nourishment." After the encounter with the artichoke, I see the likelihood that a tree, also having roots, is trying to root in Doreen. If ever there was an exercise in futility!

So how does it take in nourishment, I ask. "I can absorb it from the air and earth. And humans are so complicated."

Doreen is going to need some clarity on why a human attempting to bond with a tree is a bad idea. I ask the tree how it has affected Doreen. "I stay in the abdomen and it makes it difficult for her to digest her food. It makes her feel nauseated frequently." Plenty of motivation for Doreen to be ready to release any inclination to keep the bond between them.

The tree seems as confounded by humans as I am by it. I sense it may share my interest in understanding our difference in perspective, so I try for a conversation. I ask what is important to it as a tree that is different from what is important to humans.

"I thought that I could help to give her structure, for I understood that the purpose of wood and trees for humans is to give structure. But when they are alive, I don't understand how that structure works." I comment that human structure is very different from tree structure. "Yes."

I wonder about the tree making a distinction between one possessing a living structure and a nonliving structure. Does it view itself as having both?

I ask its name. "Cedar. I thought I understood my mission, but I am confused about how this possibly could be the right mission." I observe that the current arrangement doesn't seem to be working very well. "No."

I tell Cedar that this body is the body of Doreen, and does not belong to it. "But I understood that, as a tree gives up its consciousness to become wood, that is the mission of the tree." We are truly and completely not on the same page.

I ask Cedar if it has given up its consciousness to become wood. "No." I ask Cedar if it can find its tree body. "Yes." I ask where it is. "Still in the yard where she lived before." I offer to help Cedar to return to that tree, or to be taken to the Forests in the Light. "I would like to go to the Light because I need to reevaluate how to fulfill my mission." I ask if there are those in the Light who could help it learn. "Yes."

Before Cedar is taken to the Forests in the Light, it tells Doreen, "I can't understand you." Doreen forgives Cedar, saying she knows Cedar was trying to help. The Rescue Angels carry Cedar deep into the Forests in the Light.

Before my encounter with Cedar, when I saw the logging trucks loaded with felled, rootless trees stripped of their branches come down the highway, I would mourn for them. Now, in awe of their dedication to their mission to humans, I humbly send out my thanks for their offering of structure and support.

Nina's Foot

There appears to be a worm, and an itchy feeling in Nina's foot. "We are spreading. We would like to take up residence in the body." If somehow we have identified a parasite preparing to spread through Nina's system, I will be recommending she get to a doctor fast.

I ask the worm thing what it is. It is not, to my relief, any longer alive. This is an earthbound entity that has had life as a fungus. It attached to Nina when she was in the garden, feeling hungry and not comfortable in her own skin.

I have a question, yet unanswered, about plant life forms passing so easily from their earth life to a spirit state when they attach. It appears to have occurred with a house plant, an evergreen tree, and now a fungus.

I will not get anything helpful from the fungus. It understands it is no longer in the soil. Claims regretfully that it was happier there. It is either unaware of how it made the transition from the soil to Nina, or the transition seemed so second nature to the fungus that it went unquestioned. The fungus is delighted with my offer for it to be taken to the Fertile Soil of the Light.

Before being taken to its place in the Light, it tells Nina, "She's a great giver of light and will enrich the earth."

While my first take on fungus is the less than pleasant stuff known to cling tenaciously to the toenails of athletes and the fingernails of girls with glue-on nails, I am now challenged to expand my view to fit this new picture. Fungus: a being with a soul life, capable of giving a message of encouragement to its accidental host.

Ebony

Deborah experiences what she describes as a sense of density about her. The density tells us, "I'm immobile." So we have something that seems to be stuck. I want to know if it had a physical human body. It did not, and it recalls the light in its original place to be dark blue. Dense and dark blue does not describe anything I am familiar with, but it is early in the session and I trust things will become clearer with a few more questions.

I ask how it affects Deborah. "I keep her from dancing quite as high." So perhaps it is dragging her down with its immobility. And when did it attach to her? She was thirteen or fourteen and "She asked for help when she was in the water."

Both earthbound entities and sea creatures have attached in the water in others' sessions and I am expecting the same in this instance. I ask for its memory of the last time it was in the water. It recalls smooth, hard, nice rocks. Its name: Ebony. When asked its age, it replies that it is four million years old. I know of only one thing that could be that ancient. Deborah has attracted the attention of a rock. And a kindly one at that.

The fact of Ebony being a rock does fit very well with the immobility, and how high can you dance with a rock attached to you, even if it is only in an energetic form? Which is the real issue, not whether or not I am actually communicating with a lost rock spirit.

I tell Ebony that, as a rock, it has a place to return to amongst those other nice rocks. Ebony would like to be returned. The Rescue Angels oblige.

Gnomes, Elves And Fairies

These rare encounters all occurred for one family. The ability of members of this family to see these tiny woodland beings is traced to the lineage of the grandmother who taught her granddaughter to hunt mushrooms and shared her knowledge of forest lore with her. The great-granddaughter seems to have the gift as well.

First Encounter

When she scans her body, Lois, the granddaughter in this family, notices a brown elf-like man in the middle of her body. Her description continues. He is a small, well-proportioned man. His skin is dark, as if deeply tanned. He wears green felt-like clothing. On his feet he wears shoes that look like slippers with curled-up toes.

I invite the little man to speak and it shouts, "Get me out of here! I'm someone else (in other words, not a part of Lois) and I want to leave!"

This is new. An earthbound that can hardly wait to leave. I ask what it sees as the color of the light in its original place to clarify whether or not it is human. It tells me, "green and blue with flashes of white." That mention of green and blue is curious. There must be more to this story.

The child, Lois, had gone into the woods where her grandmother had taken her to hunt mushrooms. She was feeling lonely and frightened and looking for an escape. The little man sees her taking in, as he describes it, "the joy and the life forms in the woods."

"She carried me away from my home where I could be happy. She took me from the woods. She believed she was part of my clan." I ask who is in his clan and he tells me gnomes and fairies. "We hide when we see people."

I had not a clue as to how to help a woodland creature return to its woods, if indeed its woods still existed. I ask if it would agree to have the Rescue Angels take it into the Woodlands of the Light. It was happy to go.

Gerald With A "G"

Lois sends her daughter, Carrie, to me and I meet my second gnome.

Carrie notices a face with pointed ears and a knob of a nose floating near her. The face is deeply creased and wrinkled. Its body is chunky, with short arms and legs. The hands have knobby knuckles. It wears a blue overshirt with a belt and green knickers that fasten at the knees, and shoes that tie. It has a peaked hat that folds over to the side.

The face says in a gruff, irritated voice, "You have finally come to me!" It gives me its name: "Gerald with a G." With emphasis on the "G". It tells me it is an elf. An elf?!

Gerald tells me he is unwilling to lower himself to speak to a human. Since the conversation has already started, I press on.

When I ask if he knows if I have known any others such as he, Gerald, in a voice dripping with disdain, says that I have known one other. I am guessing that must be Lois' gnome and Gerald is of the same clan.

He expresses irritation with all the questions I ask. I explain that humans are very curious. He harrumphs, seems unimpressed, but continues to answer my questions.

Gerald attached to Carrie when she was in the dirt, playing. She had cut her face and "did not feel very attractive to her grandparents." He gives no explanation as to how he thought attaching would improve things for her, or for him.

When I ask Gerald to recall the last time he was in his own body, he describes, "Sitting on my toadstool house surveying my kingdom." He was suddenly attacked by a large hairy beast that looked like a buffalo. He blames this attack on an enemy elf that had somehow attached itself to the buffalo's horn and directed/coerced the buffalo into knocking Gerald off the toadstool.

When encouraged to look into the Light, Gerald sees "whole herds of white buffalo with many toadstools." Now I know what heaven is for gnomes. Or at least for Gerald with a "G".

Afterwards, Carrie relates that she watched Gerald be lifted up under the arms by the Rescue Angels and go huffing and kicking into the Light.

The Fairies

Carrie comes for another session. This time there appears to be a tripod shape covering her body.

The shape claims to have joined Carrie when she was a child and has caused her to feel listless, and like she does not have a place on earth where she belongs.

I ask then if the shape belongs on any place on the earth. "No. I float from place to place, like a little fairy, like a little dandelion seed."

I ask it to recall the last time it was in its own body (which is clearly not human). "I can see tall grass. And a little one sitting on a little wood chip, like a piece of pine cone, smoking a little pipe, dressed in green. It is someone I know. I am like a little fairy pet for him, following him around. He would call me his pet. He would call me a little fairy. Very tiny."

Another gnome, and this one smokes a pipe! And so small he fits on a wood chip! This is a very, very different world!

I ask the little fairy pet when it was that it found Carrie. "She travels away from home and is feeling sick and is not sure she wants to be there. But I am happy not being in any one place. I try to make her feel better. Let her feel that floating around in different places is fun. She still feels sick. I help her float in the ocean and have fun there, but she doesn't quite enjoy it as I do."

I ask the fairy-dandelion-seed-like being how it is that it left being the little pet of the gnome. "He got old and died. No one else but him seemed to notice me." So the life span of a gnome is shorter than the life span of a fairy.

I ask if there are others like it. "Yes, but they're very hard to find. But we have a way of communicating with little flashes of light. Very bright blue flashes. Not many notice the little flashing blue."

I am finding that fairies are way more agreeable than gnomes. And there has been no complaint about me being too nosey. Attempting to be polite and more fairy-like, I ask in my softest voice if it would mind answering more questions, as this was very new to me and I would like to know how to help it. It agrees.

"When you were the little pet and the little fellow wearing green died, his body didn't work any more. Does that happen to your body?"

"No. We just flash light. Just like turning on and off, we flash back. And those like us flash and help us come back." Okay. Fairies do not die.

I ask how it is that it hasn't been able to go back. "I guess I got stuck. I can see them flashing at me. I guess they're flashing quite a bit." I ask if they have been sending it a message. "Yes. Normally they don't flash that much." I ask what it is that they are trying to communicate in flashing to it. "I guess they want me to dust myself off and get back to my floating. Now that I notice, I have stayed too long in trying to help this one. Now they don't need to flash at me so much. I have to dust off . . . ."

I tell the fairy to go with our blessing and that we wish it well. And the fairy is gone.

At the end of the session, Carrie tells me the fairy's voice is very high and crystal clear, with no resonance, as if it has no need to breathe. It looks to her like a tiny rod of light with two light-filled wings attached at the top of the rod. They don't flutter when it moves. Rather, the fairy seems to move by changing the intensity of its brightness. The flights start with bursts of acceleration, and then "she" glides. A sort of fast, slow, fast, slow movement.

Being the curious human I am, I would love to be given a chance to visit again with the clans of the woodland folk.

Or to see those flashing blue lights and be reassured that the fairies are still with us.

The ET Story

Milton H. Erickson, M.D., the revered psychiatrist whose approach to his work became known as the Milton Model, recommended that the therapist go with clients, rather than lead them, in healing work. To ask the questions that allow for their story to unfold and join them in discovering the route to healing. Using this "going with" framework in spirit releasement has brought discoveries far beyond my imagination. Some of these discoveries, if I were to claim them as a product of my own, would give me big creds in the sci-fi world. Time warp, other dimensions, exploding planets, mind-control experiments. Extraterrestrials.

I have found the interests of the extraterrestrials attached to my clients to fall into a few categories. Their home has been destroyed and they are lost, looking for a safe harbor; they are performing some kind of experiment for discovery purposes; or they are intentionally doing damage.

None of the extraterrestrials I have encountered are happy with the attachment. Some are downright belligerent. Those who are sent to perform a task often view their position as a punishment. All are open to the idea of going home.

The solution to removing them is to call them out for interfering with a sentient species (apparently a big no-no in more than just sci-fi stories), and offering them that way home.

The Shimmering Green Light

The attached entity begins our contact with a disgruntled, "I don't have anything to say!"

Does it recall having a body? "No!"

How about the light it is from? "Light-green."

Does it remember how it came to be attached to Gwen when she was a baby? "I just got there. I just went there by myself." I find this hard to believe. There is too much of a sense of having been ordered rather than having made a discovery of its own. We shall see. I move on to asking how it has affected Gwen.

"I try to protect her from having weird ideas, not normal ideas. Ideas about having to achieve something."

These seem to be very normal ideas for a human. If they seem foreign to this entity, its light is a color not at all typical for an earthbound entity, and it most likely did not stumble upon Gwen. I am putting my money on this being an extraterrestrial. It won't hurt to ask.

"Where do you come from?"

"Another planet."

It tells me it was sent away as a punishment. This would explain its attitude, and appears a more genuine answer than the first one it gave.

Yes, it would like to go home. I offer to help. I do what works so very well for earthbound humans: I ask it to look up. The extraterrestrial sees a shimmering green light. Home! With its permission, I ask the Rescue Angels to take it there. Just that simply, it is gone.

Here on earth, healers often refer to green as the color of healing. They use the word, color, as a metaphor. What they are working with when they "use" green is a set of frequencies, vibrations that match the color green in the light spectrum and have a soothing, regenerating type of energy. I am mindful when an entity speaks of light—and in all of my encounters whatever their context—that we don't know until we know. How we experience the green of our light spectrum could be the same experience of green in the light spectrum of another planet or plane, or it could be something very different. What I have found thus far is that our experience of light, its significance and power, is just the tip of the iceberg when we move beyond our planet.

Green Again

Katie senses an agitation, inflammation in her lower abdomen. She tells me there is anger, tightness, holding on, a lack of nurturing coming from it. It snarls, "I'm angry!" I offer it the usual categories to describe itself. It chooses "something else." When it gives green as the color of its light, things are beginning to have a familiar ring. I ask how many of them there are.

"Just one here."

Then, the defining question: "Who sent you?"

"Controllers."

An extraterrestrial on assignment.

The interference has been going on for years. So long that Katie may not be able to distinguish between what the extraterrestrial has caused, and will no longer continue to cause, and her own issues. To free her of the confusion, I ask it to describe what it has done.

"Pain, despair, imbalance in her health, discomfort, frustration, anger, restriction, tension, tiredness, fear."

I command the controllers to remove it, according to the law of the universe that no sentient species is to be interfered with. It is withdrawn immediately. Katie confirms that it is gone. At my invitation, the Healing Angels come to heal the damage done to her.

Displaced

"We don't want you to change!" The speaker describes the "we" as a group of displaced extraterrestrials. When I ask about the color of their light, I am given:

"It was white and ended by turning black, was all closing down. Exploding. We had to get away from our planet, or wherever we were."

I ask how they were able to attach to Alex. "He was wide open. He was just so white and bright and ethereal." He was also very young. I wonder, is this the way we all begin our time on earth?

"Who sent you?"

"The dispatchers. There were thousands of us in our home, going to lots of places."

"The guardians of the universe do not allow occupation without agreement. You are invaders according to the universal laws of occupation. Would you like to be taken to be united with all the members of your planet?"

"We have become less comfortable in Alex as he has come more into his body and has less light." I begin to understand their first remark, wanting Alex not to change. They may be willing to go now.

"Call out to all your members and connect with them. Send out the message that the Rescue Angels will be arriving to take all of you to be united in your place in the Light."

The one speaking for them mumbles something about not being sure it wants to do that. I try a little persuasion.

"Look and see what it will be like."

"White light and golden light. I like the feel of the golden light."

"Send out a sensor of your energy to test it."

"The white light that I can see now more clearly is comfortable."

I take that as agreement and arrange for their transport, so to speak.

Before they are taken to their place in the Light by the Rescue Angels, they bid good-bye to Alex. I ask the Rescue Angels to gather all of them, far flung though they may be, and carry them to their place in the Light.

Gregory

Heather mentions, almost as an aside, that she has decided to stop her studies. Alarming. I wait to see what shows up in her session. Other concerns do, not this one. I take the initiative, calling out to the one who told Heather to stop her studies.

An entity responds to my query. The information tumbles out from it, some making sense if it is an earthbound entity and other indicating something very different.

It has a name: Gregory. It claims to have a body of its own. It attached to Heather because she was young and could not stop it. The light in its original place is green. It plays with her emotions. It denies it was sent by any other than itself.

Our species answers "white" to the light question. Green light is not our home energy/color. Gregory seems to be willing to continue the discussion and I need more specifics about its origins to free Heather of its influence. I encourage it to tell me more.

Gregory recalls being in pain. It gives up and "nothing good" happens. It is sent to a different area from that of everyone else. Someone high up sends it there, to a green place. "Not that great." It is a punishment. His age, really old. The year, in the future, near 3000.

Future time? The best I can make of Gregory's story is that he is not acting on his own, and he is now willing to admit it.

"Who sent you?"

"Someone bad."

"What is your job?"

"To experiment, to see how much I can control the human mind."

"What planet are you from?"

"It starts with an A. A, r something."

"I call out to the intergalactic commander of the Gregory one. Have I made clear contact with you?"

"Yes."

"Do you understand that you are interfering with a sentient species? Is that allowed? I demand that you withdraw this Gregory and all others who have been assigned to beings on this planet immediately."

It agrees.

I am incensed at its interference. I do not understand the implication of the future time Gregory has given and I am not taking any chances. I say, "All of them, in all time. Is it understood? We expect an apology."

"We're sorry."

"Depart immediately!"

I ask Heather to tell me when they are gone. I call on the Healing Angels to cleanse and heal her.

Heather, as I know clients can, has observed the entire interaction. After it was over, she described the second one I had been speaking with as The Commander. "It was tall, and was wearing all black and had no face that I could see."

Move over, Darth Vader.

Toh-lee

After we had arranged for the attached earthbound, Jonathan, to be taken to the Light, Phoebe notices something else that is not a part of her that had been hidden behind him. I call to it.

"Are you a part of Phoebe, or something or someone else?"

"I am someone else. I am inhuman."

"What kind of a being are you, what do you call yourself? Is there a place that you are from? For example, are you from earth or from somewhere else?"

"I am from another dimension, not this one."

It attached to Phoebe when, at twelve, she experienced a trauma. The entity tells me: "It was then that she was abused. I took to her. I entered her." I ask how it has affected her. "I made her world black." I ask for the color of the light in its original place. "It is not a color from here."

The mention of blackness, and then no color at all, has me wondering if this one is a dark force entity toying with us, or something I had yet to encounter. I ask, "What is the color? If you were to put it in a color spectrum, where would it be?"

"It would be past the colors into a kind of magnetic energy, but that is not true . . . . Electromagnetic."

In its mind, "Electromagnetic" seems to be a more accurate response. I have not known dark force entities to be concerned about precision. They are interested in deception. I ask another series of questions to get more clarity.

"Who sent you?"

"He is not from here, either. He is from beyond the void. He is from beyond this plane."

"If you were to give an identifier for his plane that is beyond this one, what would that identifier be?"

"A prism."

"And what is your task? What is the job you have been given by the one beyond this plane?"

"To attach to those of light. To, I would say, demoralize. To war with them."

"And what happens to you if you do not do this work?"

"I cannot go home."

"Who is it who has told you you cannot go home?"

"The one who sent me."

"Do you like what you are doing?"

"It is pathetic."

"Can you stop doing this thing that is pathetic?"

"I suppose I can. I hadn't thought about it."

"Would you like us to help you?"

Skeptical, it asks, "How can you help me?"

"Would you like us to?"

"Yes."

Counting on the angels to be able to handle the situation, I say, "I call on the Warrior Angels who have capacities in all dimensions to stand around this field. I call on the Rescue Angels to cast a protective net of light, mesh of light, capsule of light, inescapable, impermeable, protective around this one. And fill the capsule with light."

I ask the extraterrestrial, "How does that feel, little one?"

"It feels strange."

"Is it light that you recognize?"

"Yes."

"What did the one beyond this plane who sent you tell you would happen if this light touched you?"

"That I would never again be allowed to return to where I am from. I would have failed, and I would forever be cast out."

I make note of the similarity between this threat and what dark force entities will use to manipulate and control their victims. I continue with the questions used to liberate a dark force entity once it is encapsulated in light, assuming that will work to help what is beginning to look like an extraterrestrial as well.

"What did that one tell you light would feel like?"

"It would feel like a burning sensation inside my body."

"It would burn you?"

 "Yes."

"Are you burning?"

"A little."

"How does that burning feel?"

 "It feels all right, I suppose."

"Not bad?"

 "No."

"It seems you were not told the truth about this light. Maybe you were not told the truth about not being able to go home, either. What did this one tell you you would find if you looked deep inside?"

 "A hole. A deep well."

"Maybe you should check. Go inside, all the way in, and tell me what you find."

"I find my center."

"What is in it?"

"Such beautiful things! A lake and a river and lots of beauty."

This is new. I expected it to find a spark of light in its center. The entity seems to be pleased with what it has discovered. I decide to help it explore what it has found.

"Does this look familiar to you?"

"Yes, it's my home."

"What is the land called that this home is in?"

"Pah-thag-ree-ance, something like that."

"And so you have been home all of this time?!"

Laughing, "Oh, don't say it like that!"

"Is that a wonderful thing?"

"It's a terrible thing, because it's been here the whole time."

"And you have been used."

"I have been abused . . . and used. For all this time."

"How long has this been going on?"

"For long."

"Would you like to be returned to your home?"

"Very, very much."

"Would you claim for the Light?"

"Hm. Okay."

It appears I have thrown this being a curve. It seems game to claim for the Light, even though claiming this does not resonate with the being the way it does for a dark force entity who has reached this point in an interaction.

I explain, "This is our way of assuring that you can be taken safely."

"Yes. Thanks."

I decide to see if we can get a more developed concept of what this being is. I ask, "Is there a name that we can call you?"

"Toh-lee."

"For Phoebe, would you describe your body, as you enjoy it, in your home?"

"I am long and thin and lean and I am like . . . purple. I am purple."

"Can you compare your form to Phoebe's form? How is it different from hers?"

"She is very soft, and I am lighter than she."

"What is your sensing system like?"

"I can see beyond into the heavens and into the space between. I can see everything."

Amazing! I wonder if the Rescue Angels, whom I know to be light beings, are viewed similarly by it. I ask, "Do you notice the Rescue Angels?"

"Yes."

"How do they appear to you?"

"They appear as light." I guess I should have expected that.

"Before they take you, is there anything you would like to say to Phoebe, anything you would like her to know?"

"I am sorry that I abused you and that I used your body for my own purposes. I am going to the Light now. Maybe I can help the others like me."

Phoebe is reluctant to forgive it. To encourage her, I tell Phoebe, "The importance of forgiving this one is to break the bond so you are free." With effort, she does so.

In other instances of discovering an attached extraterrestrial, it has been possible to contact the extraterrestrial's controller and do what Toh-lee hopes to accomplish. Expecting to do so here, I say, "I call to the commander of this one. This is a sentient species that you have invaded. According to the universal laws, invasion of this species is not to be allowed. Do you understand what I am saying?"

"Yes. I do understand."

"And so, I demand that this cease immediately and that you recall all the ones you have implanted in this species. Are you in agreement?" There is a long pause. I wait.

"I do not wish to be, but I am."

All that remains is to send Toh-lee on its way.

"And so, little one, go with our blessing. I call on the Rescue Angels to carry this one safely to its true home. I ask this in the name of the Light." Phoebe watches as Toh-lee is taken.

Part 3: Soul Fragment Retrieval

Soul Fragment Retrieval

Soul retrieval, shamanism, is an ancient practice enjoying a revival in alternative therapy circles today. In shamanism's original form, such as in the Andean tradition, shamans are healers who serve their community in many ways. One of the healing methods they employ is to "travel" in a dream state to locate and recover the lost soul fragments of their patients. The shaman then returns the fragments to their owners and in this way, restores the patients to wholeness.

Soul fragment retrieval is a form of this shamanistic event. It differs from the traditional practice of shamanism in that clients are active participants in the process. Clients are assisted to notice what is missing within them and to locate those lost parts of themselves. These separated fragments are asked if they would like help to come back to the client and, with the help of the angels, are returned. Finally, the client witnesses the reuniting of the soul fragments that had been displaced.

Soul fragment retrieval also extends beyond retrieval to include the release and sending back of soul fragments of others that have become embedded in the affected one.

"Sharing" Hearts

There is a belief common in our culture which encourages the "giving a piece of our heart" to express love and commitment. The problem with this romantic notion is that it burdens the recipients, causing them to carry the weight of another's soul, and eliminates access of the givers to a part of their own soul/consciousness. We are, in effect, encouraging soul fragmentation and implantation.

How is it possible to love "wholeheartedly" if what we have to love with is no longer whole?

Beyond the romantic notion is the possessiveness involved in placing a soul fragment in the one who is loved. It is truly a way of owning that person, and is not always done with the agreement of the recipient. Mothers and lovers seem to be the biggest offenders.

Soul Fragmentation

It can happen that when we experience a trauma, we fragment, sending out pieces of ourselves to find safety. Fragmentation can also be the result of a wonderfully overwhelming, ecstatic experience. In either event, the result is an emotional emptiness. A feeling of being somehow vacant inside. Understandable, because an essential part of our consciousness has vacated.

I stumbled across my first experience with soul fragmentation when I reunited with a friend several years after we had met in a meditation class. She had dropped out of the classes, while I continued. She had invited me and a few other friends from the class over for a bit of a reunion. We spent a pleasant afternoon catching up, and, as we were on our way out the door, I twisted my ankle.

Charlene brought me back in and sat me down to give my ankle some time to recover. It was just the two of us there. My curiosity got the better of me, and I asked why she hadn't continued with the classes. Charlene talked about the last class she attended, and, as she told her story, I remembered seeing what had happened without understanding how it had affected her.

The meditation had been an intense experience for all of us. For Charlene, it had been, as she described it, an encounter with The All That Is. Ecstatic. I had seen her collapse at the end of the meditation and truthfully had not thought much of it because, every now and again, someone would pass across that "wake/sleep border" in a meditation and come close to falling out of the chair.

What had happened for Charlene was an exponential measure beyond slipping out of her seat. She had become so overwhelmed with the immensity of that encounter that her soul had completely fragmented. Vacated. Since the fragmentation, she had lived with an emotional emptiness that left her without the ability to experience even the simplest pleasure. Music had no meaning, feelings of friendship or love were just gone. She struggled to reconstruct her capacity to experience emotion. After great effort, Charlene managed to regain a small portion of what she had had before.

Without thinking about how I would do it I "looked," and discovered, to my surprise, that I could "see" those missing fragments, sort of "out there." If I could see them, I knew I could get her to them. I asked Charlene if she would let me help, and, with what I consider a humbling amount of trust, she agreed. I "took" her to where I had found them and held both Charlene and the fragments in my awareness as she gathered them all back. Then I made sure she came all the way back into the room.

I tell this as a cautionary tale. It is very possible to have too much of a good thing. Experimenting with higher states of consciousness without some guidance can be devastatingly overwhelming.

Traumatic Events

If it has happened that you are the victim of an extreme trauma, the message is that there is the possibility of help and recovery. Souls do fragment when we encounter violence and abuse. With the help of the angels, there can be healing and restoration.

More Tales To Tell

Every story of soul fragment retrieval is as individual as the fragments that have become lost or entangled. Some inadvertently, some with purpose. What follows is a sampling of the many I have encountered.

Restraint

There is a sensation of numbness in Barb's right shoulder. We explore that, Barb saying that the source of the numbness seems tired. It has been with this young woman, barely nineteen, since she was sixteen. I ask about the color of its light and am given "purple." Okay, purple. I have no idea what that means. I move on and ask how it affects Barb. It restrains her.

I guess that since it claims to be tired, it would be interested in having its situation rectified. I will need to know more to help both the entity and Barb, and ask the being attached to her about the two things that usually work to jog a lost soul's memory: if it has been alive in its own body, and if it remembers its name.

There is none of the confusion earthbounds sometimes experience in recalling their earth life. It tells me without hesitation: it is Barb's mother. A fragment of her consciousness attached to the daughter, wanting to look out for her and yet tired of the responsibility.

A simple negotiation can clear this up. First the mother. Would she like this fragment of herself returned to her? No problem there. I ask Barb if she is ready to send this fragment back to her mother. Absolutely!

Barb releases the fragment, the Rescue Angels carrying it back to her mother, freeing both of them to enjoy a less burdened, more open relationship.

Sticky Strings

Al feels rubbery, sticky things, hooks and strings on himself. He seems uncomfortable with them being there. I wonder if those strings attached to Al have more to do with what is missing from him than what is attached to him. I ask Al to check and see if there are any strings or cords or ropes going out from this area. He sees cords. Al has missing fragments at the ends of those cords, I am sure.

I ask Al to chose a cord, then ask an angel to go with him to find where it leads. He finds it leads to his ex-wife. I see the possibility that it would feel sticky to be tied to an ended relationship. I call on the Rescue Angels to carry the soul fragment that belongs to Al back to him, fitting it in place and sealing it in.

Al finds five more soul fragments he has placed in past loves. Then one "little one" he had tucked into a male friend. The Healing Angels cleanse all of them and, with Al's agreement, the Rescue Angels return them to him.

The Green Hole In The Stomach

The entity attached to Hanna gives her a piece of advice: "Be healthy, eat, not drink." Hanna gets the message—she needs to take care of herself and cut down on the drinking. Good advice, yet who needs her own resident internal nag? And how did Hanna get a hole in her stomach?

I take on the one handing out the advice first. It gives us the current year as the one it recalls, not a date in the past. An indication that Hanna has a soul fragment attached to her. Friendly or no, it is not a part of her and needs to be sent back to its owner.

We discover that this is a fragment of Don, a close friend and mentor of sorts. It was concern for Hanna that caused the placement of the fragment, and her insecurity that provided the opening. He recognizes that, despite his good intentions, he has invaded Hanna. Not helpful for her, a form of tethering for him. He wants his fragment back.

Hanna could have sent Don's soul fragment back to him with only her decision not to keep it. It was just more harmonious to have them both be in agreement. She sends it back and he accepts it.

Now for that green hole. I help Hanna follow out the cords she finds leading out of her stomach, each one attached to a fragment of her soul.

Soul fragments that have left because of trauma often need help and reassurance that it is safe to be returned. In this case, when I ask Hanna's if they are ready to be returned to her, they are in agreement. The Healing Angels are called to clean each of them, and the Rescue Angels to return them to Hanna. Hanna watches as the angels fit them back into the space they left.

Thoughtforms

"Don't fill me up!" The one that says this describes itself as an energy that Rachel acquired by collecting many mass thoughtforms—aggregates of thoughts that form beliefs and seem to take on lives of their own—and keeping them in her stomach.

I cannot begin to imagine the burden this roiling glob of disjointed thoughts is creating for Rachel. I am hoping we can remove them by sending the thoughts back to their source, as if they are soul fragments.

I ask if there are cords or threads or strands running out from the glob. Rachel tells me she sees many. This should work. I ask her to follow one out, in company with the Rescue Angels. It leads to Rachel's mother.

First things first. Mothers do not belong in daughters. I have a conversation with the soul fragment implanted in Rachel. It verifies it is a part of Rachel's mother. She started to weave and implant this in Rachel in early infancy.

I suspect that the weaving and implanting story means it will be futile to ask Rachel's mother to end something she so carefully plotted. It will have to be Rachel who makes the decision to end the invasion.

Rachel would like the implantation removed. The Rescue Angels do so, lifting it out and carrying it back to her mother.

I call to all the pieces attached to Rachel that are not her, asking if they are in agreement for the Rescue Angels to carry them to their true homes. I also ask if she is in agreement. Yes. The clean up can begin.

The Rescue Angels gather up all the thoughtforms, disconnecting them from Rachel. Rachel watches as they are carried away. She tells me that it was like lifting a rock and having insects scurry out from underneath. Good to have them gone.

Reclaiming

I begin by asking Louise that, if she imagined herself to be a pie, what percentage of the pie she would have in her body. "Three quarters." There is another quarter of her soul self that she has sent out. There is retrieval work to be done.

I call out to the missing quarter of Louise and ask if these parts are ready to be returned to her. Louise's response: there is just one piece, with "the one she loves." Tears trail down Louise's face.

We locate it with Louise's former boyfriend. He is not interested in letting it go.

"If I return it, I will lose her."

"We are meant to love with a whole heart, not to imprison a part of someone. Are you willing to allow Louise to love with a whole heart and love freely, whether she chooses you or not?"

"She is my only love."

"Ah, yes, dear one, but you have had many loves and will have many more. You have yourself been anchored down by holding this piece of her. She wishes to be free and wishes you to be free as well. Being free sends out a signal to the ones you have covered your ears to, so they know you hear them. Does your love give to her or take from her?"

"It takes from her."

"Is that love, something that takes?"

"It is not."

"It is not love, but fear, that has you holding on. Would you believe me if I said you do not need to be afraid? There is one with you who loves you unconditionally and is with you all the time. Do you see that one?"

"Yes. It is telling me it is not good to hold on to the part of Louise. It is showing me what it does to me to hold on. It shows me that it makes me afraid."

"And so, you are frightening yourself."

He agrees to lovingly release the part of Louise that he holds. Louise agrees to take this part back. I call on the Healing Angels to wash the part completely free of the fear it has been coated in and the Rescue Angels to gently return it to her, fitting it into place and sealing it in with light.

Part 4: Dark Force Entities

Prisoners Of Darkness

They describe themselves as creatures of the dark. They serve the darkness out of fear for their existence, imprisoned in the illusion that they have no other choice. They trust no one. Expect excruciating punishment if they fail in their assignment. Consider that the greatest threat is to be touched by the light, believing it will burn and destroy them.

It is no wonder they try so desperately to escape notice when they are found. When they are called out, there is a last ditch attempt to intimidate, using the same kind of tactics that have them trapped. And no matter how many times they witness their brothers of the darkness discover they have been imprisoned by deception, they will not trust that light will free them.

My first encounter with dark force entities came as a huge revelation. I had been working with earthbound attachments for some time, not aware that dark force entities existed. I held the view that belief in the existence of evil forces was an outdated concept. I recognized people as capable of acting in harmful ways out of fear and need. Their anger and violence merely attempts to find a way to survive in a threatening world. Mankind and nothing else the source of hurt and destruction.

Then I found the books of William Baldwin, Ph.D., and Judith Baldwin. First, *Healing Lost Souls,* then *Spirit Releasement Therapy.* This was the beginning of my experience with a hugely less benevolent universe. I would finish reading a chapter of *Spirit Releasement Therapy* and shortly after, someone would show up for a session with exactly the situation I had read about. It was becoming increasingly unnerving to face the evil in its own right that I now had no choice but to accept as a reality. It clearly was time to deepen my abilities if I planned on continuing to help my clients. I turned to the Baldwin's training on spirit releasement for help.

One of my grandmother's favorite sayings, "The proof of the pudding is in the tasting," must affect me more than I realize. Because once again, just as it had happened in the training seminar on earthbound entities, I was the subject of a demonstration for the release of a dark force entity.

I felt it lodged in my forehead. It was causing some serious discomfort. I experienced it as completely separate from me. It disdainfully called me a foolish, foolish girl for allowing it to attach. It's job: to interfere with my work.

It was convinced the light was going to destroy it, amazed when it didn't. And apparently had been paying attention to what had been happening in my sessions with clients because it asked that the other dark force entities it knew of also be encapsulated in light and saved as well. With my inner vision, I watched as they were called by it. Tiers and tiers of them were wrapped in light. Very much like we were in the center of a stadium. Then I watched as they were all taken into the Light. If I had had any doubts about how effective this work is, they were completely erased.

Encounters

My encounters with dark force entities played out in so predictable a way that I began to wonder if any sense of self, of who they uniquely are, remained in them.

With that first inquiry, asking if they are a part of my client, or something or someone else, they often throw out some sort of threat. Growling, or hissing, refusing to answer, or going for a statement they hope will intimidate. "We hate you!" for example. "Get out of here!" is another. Even though reluctant to continue the conversation, once engaged, every last one of them keeps on going.

I ask a simple question. "Who sent you?" They seem to assume I know they are not acting on their own. Many would tell me they could not say who sent them for fear of punishment. Specifically, being sent to a place they call "the pit." I ask about this place. They speak of burning, and terrifying sounds. The most colorful description I have been given: "They will come with much noise and fire and push us down into the darkness."

Often, the dark force entities would provide a description of who controls them. Not one controller has a name of its own. The Dark One, The Chief, The Boss, One Who Is Above All, The One Who Lives In Darkness, The Evil Ones. A dragon, a huge bat, a thing that breathes fire through its nostrils, a shadowy figure on a horse wielding a spear, a fearful thing who cracks a whip. Figures who people nightmares. I suspect they are images borrowed from my clients' imaginations. I know that dark force entities trade in the currency of fear.

I have two more questions for them: have you ever been alive in a physical body of your own, and what is the color of the light in your original place? The answer to the former is undoubtedly "no," with an occasional attempt to finesse the answer by claiming they own the body they have attached to. The latter is some form of dark, or no light. An occasional desperate stab at "painting" themselves white, or purple, or yellow, thinking they can deceive me into thinking they aren't what they are. The ones who have tried the color disguise say things like, "See? I'm white," or "I made that purple." It seems they are so used to dealing in lies, they miss how completely they are giving themselves away.

They know that, if I know they claim the darkness, they are probably in trouble. This will be the time they will make some statement about how powerful the darkness is, and how powerful they are, aiming to be as fear-producing as they can.

Fortunately, I know there are angels, beings of the Light, standing in the wings. Light does not trade in the dark ones' currency of fear.

Now there are discoveries to be made that will be critical to the healing of my client: what made it possible for the dark force entity to attach, what job has it been given, what harm has it done. Most of the responses will be truthful.

With the preliminary work done, it is time to begin the process of freeing my client and restoring the dark one to the Light. Here, in the stories of Patricia, Brian and Paula, is a sampling of how that occurs.

Patricia

When Patricia scans her body at the beginning of the session, she tips her head away from the form of a wolf's head, its teeth snapping towards her ear. She tries to pull away from the exposed teeth.

I ask the wolf if it has ever been alive in its own physical body. "You are not worthy to ask that question! You need to go away!" A typical attempt by a dark force entity to get me to back off. I ask when it attached to Patricia. She was four, feeling alone and hungry and isolated. I ask how it has affected her. "I keep her on edge and under control, like she is subservient to my pack." It tells me that it rules the pack, as if they are wolves.

"There are others of my kind. We are a collection of rulers who gather souls for our pack."

I ask who sent them to Patricia. "We spread fear, but there is one we fear as well. He is both a wolf and a snake."

I ask how it can have animal forms when it doesn't have a body of its own. It tells me that they are shapeshifters and can shift to the shape that is most effective.

"And so, you can look like the shape, even though you aren't the shape?"

"Yes. We are malleable, depending on the need. Depending on the fear, to frighten."

When I ask what they are really, not what shape they assume to inspire fear, it does not answer. I ask, "Would you be fooled by the same thing that you use to fool others?"

"That is how he rules."

For emphasis, I ask if it would really be fooled by what it uses to fool people.

"Hm. It is a thought I had not entertained."

I ask what happens if it fails. "The snake will bite and sting and hurt."

I point out that it isn't really a snake. "Um, that was what was told to me."

"Who was it that told you that?"

"I do not know the truth of that being."

"I wonder what the truth of that being is. I wonder what *your* truth is."

"I am frightened as well."

"And alone."

"Yes."

I ask if the members of its pack care about it. "They seem to focus only on keeping the leader satisfied."

"Because they are afraid of him? Of this illusion?"

"It seems that is closer to the truth."

I ask again, "What is your truth?"

"I want to be loved and I felt I could win that love by obedience."

"Did someone tell you that love needs to be earned? Who was it that told you such a thing?"

"This one who has erased my memory from all but this service."

"Did the snake/wolf one erase your memory?"

"I can only recall the service to this one."

I encourage it to recall, and see what it sees. It asks me to protect it while it recalls. I call the Rescue Angels to encapsulate it in protective light.

"How does the light feel, little one?

"It feels safe. It is not destroying me."

"What did the snake/wolf one tell you the light would be like?"

"It was to be feared, that it is a method of destruction."

"Are you being destroyed?"

"No. I am being sheltered."

"What were you told you would find if you went inside, to your very center?"

"An endless pit of darkness."

I encourage it to go to its center and notice what is there.

"A sparkling core of light that is secure and protected."

I encourage it to watch the core of light.

"It expands and joins with the light of the cocoon and encompasses all of it with love and peace."

"Did you have to win the love and the peace?"

"No. I simply had to allow it to expand."

It has recognized the light within it. We are one step away from this dark force entity's return to the Light. I ask, "Will you claim for the Light?" It does, willingly.

I ask, "How does the light feel?"

"It feels like coming home."

I am aware that a dark force entity, newly returned to the Light, has not completely abandoned the self-interest it has used to survive in an ugly world. I use this self-interest as the avenue to free even more souls.

I tell this one, "Shortly, the Rescue Angels will take you to your place in the Light, where there is work for you to do, and learning, and then you will be able to choose your new work in the Light. But before that can happen, there is work for you to do. There must be recompense, there must be a balance, for you are responsible for everything you have done. Do you understand?"

"Yes."

"Would you like to begin that recompense now?"

"Yes."

It is amazing to me that this discussion occurs in the same way with every dark force entity I have assisted in returning to the Light.

As a first act of recompense, I ask it to call those who are under it to the field of light (established around us by the Warrior Angels at the beginning of the session). It tells me that there are a few. They come and the Rescue Angels encapsulate each one in light.

I instruct the newly returned entity to tell them to claim for the Light. This is done.

It calls those at its level to the field. These are the ones it has called the collection of rulers. These are encapsulated in light. It tells them to claim for the Light, which they do.

It had mentioned that there were "collections" under these, and I ask the newly returned entity to call the others under these. They come and claim for the Light when it tells them. There are hundreds of them.

Now it calls to the ones above the collection of rulers. It tells me the one that it knows has come, and that there are three others who are watching the events. I call on the Rescue Angels to encapsulate those three in light as well. When it tells these four to claim for the Light, they first "overcome their confusion" and then willingly claim for the Light.

It calls the ones above these to the field. Two arrive. "They have come, and by this action their entire field of power has been short-circuited." It observes that when these two claim for the Light, their ferocity is reduced to "the smallest of little sparks." It tells me, "By their inactivation, there appears to be a field of ashes below them that they had believed were soldiers in their powerful force. They were merely illusions."

As one last act of recompense, I ask again how it has affected Patricia, expecting a more honest answer than the one it gave before it reclaimed the Light.

"We made her believe that it is important for the mass thoughtform of fear and separation to be accepted in her generation. We have perpetuated the belief that she must earn the love of her father and that his approval of her depends on her actions. We have produced feelings of anxiety and panic attacks and let them bubble up through her psyche and develop unchecked. By having her always pulling away from the bared teeth, we have kept her attention away from the beauty of the earth and of her surroundings. She needs to know that her cat has interfered with our activities and, from this point of view in the Light, we can see that he has been a key factor in creating joy in her life and love. She is very lucky. She has been using that affirmation and, in truth, she has been able to overcome much of the fear that we had worked to perpetuate. From this point of view we can see that we were failing in our control."

The acknowledgment of Patricia's cat as a counter to the dark force entities' work comes as a surprise. I have suspected there is more to cats than companionship. They are certainly little healers in their own right.

I want to recognize this one's willingness to give itself completely over to the Light. I offer it to choose a new name for itself, as a being who has claimed for the Light.

"Tex, which represents the state in which Patricia had a glimpse of universal love. It is also a play on words, as it is text messages that Patricia exchanges that bring her humor and communication with her friends. (It spells out T-e-x.) And Tex conveys a feeling of power in the American language. Although I now see that power is not important, it was the entire goal of my beingness prior to my awakening to the Light."

"And so," I say, before the Rescue Angels carry all of the encapsulated entities to their place in the Light, "this one will be known as Tex of the Light."

There is another task for the Rescue Angels. I ask them to gather up all the lost souls who were freed when the dark force entities attached to them were encapsulated in light, and carry the lost souls safely to their place in the Light. Then I call on the beings of the light communities who ameliorate energy to gather up all the residue from our work so that it can be restructured, rewoven, reharmonized.

Patricia, released from the influence of the dark force entities, is still in need of cleansing and healing. The Healing Angels come and begin the work that will continue until she is free of all residue from the attachment and restored by the healing energy of the Light.

Brian

Brian notices a throbbing sensation in his eye. There is also a sensation of the source of the pain trying to withdraw so it will avoid being noticed.

I invite the one trying to withdraw to speak. Using Brian's voice, it gives out a hissing sound. I ask the hissing one if it has been alive in its own body. It replies in a deep, angry voice, "We resent you asking that." I repeat the question. It answers, "No." I ask for the color of the light in its original place. "We have darkness." I ask how old Brian was when it, and the others, attached to him. "Eight." The vulnerability that allowed them in: "seeing the father withdraw from the family home."

"And how have you affected him?"

"We try to bring him down. We try to keep him from going into crowds and having fun and playing with other people."

"So you have caused him to be isolated?"

"We try to isolate him, but we are not very successful."

"What happens to you if you are not successful?"

"Our work will be tallied up in the future and if we are not successful, we will be burned and branded. Burned with hot pokers."

"When the tallying happens?"

"When my assignment here is over."

I notice the sudden shift in the discussion from "we" who will be burned to "my assignment." The entity has come out from behind the screen, no longer presenting itself as an anonymous member of a group. Now we can have a real conversation. I ask when the assignment will be over.

"I'm not really sure. It might be when the Brian One's life is over. I'm not really sure."

"They were not very specific about when these terrible things would happen?"

"No."

"Have you ever experienced burning before?"

"No."

"Do you know anyone of your kind who has?"

"No. I have heard the noise of it." (This is said with hesitation.)

"What was it that was burning when you heard the noise?"

"It was, uh, I don't know."

"Only the sound?"

"It was crackling and hissing."

"That sounds a lot like wood to me."

"Could it be?"

"Are you made of wood?"

"No."

"Has anything you are made of, have you seen anything like that burn?"

"No. Not me. I've seen wood burn, but not me."

"Is wood of the same substance that you are?"

"No."

"Do you have a body?"

"No."

"How are you going to burn if you don't have a body?"

"I don't know. I believed it."

"It seems you have, because you have been acting in fear that it will. But it is beginning to look like you have been living in fear of something that will not happen because it cannot. (I pause for a moment, giving the dark force entity time to digest this.) Would you like our help?"

"Yes!"

"Do you feel you need to hiss anymore?"

"No."

It is subdued, but not captured. I call on the Warrior Angels to stand around this field and then call on the Rescue Angels to encapsulate it in light and, as the dark force entity's first experience of the return from darkness, to fill the capsule with light. I ask it how the light feels.

"It feels soothing and like the truth. Like it's really there."

"What did the one who would tally tell you the light would be like?"

"It would burn and destroy."

I ask what they told it that it would find if it looked inside. "That is not to be done."

"They told you, 'Do not do it'? Any reason why?"

A long pause. "Hm."

"I think I know why."

"They did not say."

"I think they didn't want you to know what you would find there—which would be very bad for them, but very good for you. Go look! Go all the way inside and tell me what you find that they didn't want you to know about."

"A little speck of light!"

I encourage it to watch the speck of light and tell me what happens. "It is growing with my attention. And there is no change in the feeling of peace and harmony and truth that I was feeling. There is no change at all!"

I ask if it would claim for the Light. "Yes! I gladly claim for the Light."

In recognition of the entity's new status, I say, "It is recorded that this one claims for the Light!" I ask it how that feels.

"It feels like the right thing to do, the right action. It feels like being rewarded for the right action rather than working for fear and punishment."

As the beginning of its recompense, the entity calls the ones at its level to the field so they can be encapsulated in light. They claim for the Light. It calls the ones above these, many, many. They claim for the Light. It calls the ones above these and they claim for the Light. Then another level. They claim for the Light. Then another level. They claim for the Light. There are five in this group. Then the next level. They claim for the Light. Then the next level. There are two. They claim for the Light. I ask to speak to one of them. One of them agrees.

"Are there those above you who control you?"

"There is one."

"Call this one."

"It is moving slowly like a slug, slithering, not entirely encompassed in the capsule." I call Archangel Michael and his Warrior Angels to the field and ask them to encapsulate it in light completely so that it notices it has been encapsulated in light and that there is no escape. "Yes. That was effective."

I ask the one who was using the illusion of the slug how the light feels. "It is a surprise. It is cool and soothing."

"And you were informed that it was. . . ?"

"I felt that it was only eternal damnation. That there were only flames of burning fire."

"That would go on for eternity?"

"Yes."

"Now what do you know?"

"There is love and forgiveness."

I ask the controller one to claim for the Light. This is done.

As a last act of recompense, I ask the reclaimed entity that was attached to Brian to describe how it has affected Brian so he will know the influence he no longer lives under. This will be the beginning of Brian's healing.

"I've been the one that pulls you down and tries to sap your physical strength and vitality. And tells you that you are not good enough. That makes you feel that only through subjugating yourself to others that you will be loved. I've tried to hide from you your true power and the beauty of your inner being. I want to release you to have your full strength and power and light for the personal use of your soul. For I see now that my assignment was all a lie and that it was destructive to you and that true power and love are only possible in the Light. There is no need to punish yourself mentally or emotionally for who you truly are, for your true being is very powerful. It is no longer necessary for you to look towards your father's model as a model for your life. His influence was necessary to bring you here. It is not at all necessary for your life's work. And I am truly sorry for having tried to interfere with your life's work by following my puny assignment that has no meaning and has no future. For it was my mistake to follow that lie."

I ask Brian if he can forgive the entity. He does this, and by this, releases any remaining ties to the entity. The Rescue Angels then carry all the encapsulated entities to their place in the Light, and the Healing Angels are called to cleanse and heal Brian.

Paula

Paula sees gray shapes that flit across her eyes. I call to the one in charge of the gray shapes. This one appears as a soldier. It tells me it was planning on letting "the underling" do the talking.

"The underling" statement is typical of the language dark force entities use.

Paula's session was one of my early encounters with dark force entities, and I used a more basic method to deal with what I had discovered—I asked the Rescue Angels to encapsulate the entity in light, fill the capsule with light, and squeeze the capsule so the dark force entity had no choice but to experience the light.

Frantically, it calls out, "It's tight! It's light! I like it darker! This is too bright! I have to draw my sword and cut through it, but I can't get to it!"

"What have you been told about the light?"

"To avoid it!"

"You are no longer hiding in the dark. You have been found, and now you are talking to us. What will they do to you?"

"Oh, that bad place!"

"What will happen to you there?"

"I will be punished."

"Are you being punished?"

"Well, not yet. I've just been caught."

"Is the light burning you?"

"No. It's just bright!"

Going with the illusion he has given that he is a soldier, I tell him to put his toe in the light and see how it feels.

135

"Well, it feels okay. . . ."

"Notice what is happening to your edges."

"They're melting and getting round."

"What have you been told is at your core?"

"An orange."

"Are you telling the truth?"

He admits that he is lying, laughing.

"What have you been told about the Light?"

"That it will destroy me."

"Are you being destroyed?"

"No. I'm being squeezed like an orange (laughing) until all the juice is gone. You are squeezing me, by the way."

"Is your juice gone?"

"No. But you are squeezing me. I have rounded edges."

I suggest he should go and look to see if they have told him the truth about what is at his core.

He laughs about looking in the dark.

It is not clear to me whether it is attempting to taunt, or to deflect. Either way, I have had enough. I tell the soldier to go and look and that this is not silliness and if it thinks it is, I will ask the Rescue Angels to add more light to its capsule. Firmly, I say, "Go to your core and report."

"There is a little something there that is not dark. It seems to have a little flicker."

"What flickers?"

"A light. Maybe I am not a soldier. Maybe I'm acting a part."

"Do you want to be a soldier?"

"Uh-unh! No!"

"Look at the light in your center, little one."

"It is coolish, not burning. They said it would burn."

"And you would be destroyed."

"Yes they did!"

"Why would you follow the commands of someone who lied to you like this?"

"Because I had no choice, that's why."

"You are a being of light. This light is your connection to Source. You are a godly being and have choice in the Light, to choose light or darkness. You can offer the Light to your friends as well. Put out a call to the ones under you."

It calls them, telling them it can offer them the Light. The Rescue Angels encapsulate them in light. It tells them to choose for the Light individually, not as a legion.

It notices a second legion that is not coming. It calls it to the field and the Rescue Angels encapsulate all those in the legion in light. It notices there is one left. The Rescue Angels encapsulate it in light. It sees another. This one too is encapsulated.

Then, at my urging, the soldier makes the claim that it chooses for the Light, and invites all the legions under it to choose for the Light, telling them, "If you choose for the Light, you will be free in the Light."

There are more souls to be freed. I ask it to call the ones it knows at its level, and, as they come, they are encapsulated in light. The ones under their control are called and encapsulated. I suggest they all find their spark of light inside, their key to freedom. This is done.

The ones who are above the soldier, all the way to The Director, are called to the field and encapsulated in light. Once again, the soldier offers the choice of the Light. It confirms that all, including The Director, accept the offer.

I tell the soldier, "You have begun your recompense and all of this is recorded in your favor."

Before it is taken to its place in the Light, it apologies to Paula for causing her what it calls inconveniences. "Too many to mention because there were a lot of us working."

I am about to call it out for saying their actions were mere inconveniences when it tells me it is taking a moment to go back and look at that. "We were to search out and destroy good feelings."

To finalize the removal of their connection to her, I ask Paula if she can forgive them. When this is done, the Rescue Angels carry all of them to their place in the Light. The Healing Angels come to cleanse and heal Paula.

Portals: Laura's Story

One of the more profitable means of energy gathering for dark force entities is to establish an opening, a portal into their victim.

The opening is made by a dark force entity who finds a break or weakness in the energy field, or aura, surrounding a person. The dark force entity uses this as an entry point for itself and then establishes a permanent opening. This allows easy entry for others of its kind. The portal is created by a dark force entity who is higher in the ranks and has more experience with attachments. The higher-ranked dark force entities are more capable of hiding as well and are usually the last to be uncovered, shoving lesser-ranked dark force entities out in front to avoid discovery, as is the case in Laura's story.

Multiple dark force entities were discovered in Laura's session. The first encountered, when asked how it was able to attach to Laura, tells us it came in through an open portal. "I walked right in. I waltzed in." It gives us a description of the portal: round, like the portal in a ship.

There are several other dark force entities identified and encapsulated in light, and none of them claiming responsibility for creating the portal, before one of them points out an entity who has been around and watching, calling it "Someone Else." This is enough of an identifier for me to engage the one who has been around and watching in a conversation.

I ask this one about the color of its light. "I have made it purple." An obvious dodge. Light is the color it is, not what the entity makes it.

I ask, "What color did your light start out as?"

"Blackness." This, I believe.

We have begun a truthful discussion. It gives up that it attached to Laura when she was two years old. "She was so young and innocent."

When asked how it has affected her, it responds, "Oh, I have just done everything. Can't sleep, she's mean."

I ask about the portal, if it is its creation. "Oh, yes! And didn't it work well! (chuckling) I did a really good job on that one."

"The angels have blocked it now, haven't they? Look."

"Why did they go and do that?! We're not going to have company any more. Why did they go and ruin such a good thing? We had all kinds of people coming and going. Mainly coming. Not too many people going. At least not of their free will."

"How many are there now?"

"A few score."

"Who sent you?"

"The Evil Ones."

"And what is your job?"

"Havoc. Ruin. And those horsemen, you know. The apocalypse horsemen. All of that."

"Very colorful!"

"Yes. Goes with my purple color."

We are back to the purple story and away from accepting blame for the greater damage it has caused by establishing the portal. "Did they instruct you to establish the portal?"

"They did."

"It is closed and you have failed."

"But I had it!"

"What do they do to ones who fail?"

"We get cast aside in the pit."

"Are you in trouble?"

"Yes, I'm in trouble, but maybe they won't find out."

"Are they watching?"

"I don't think they're watching right now, but they might notice."

"What happens when they do?"

"I'll get tossed in the pit."

"They are going to find out. Would you like us to help you?"

"Help? No one has ever offered to help! I've always given the help to those other people causing havoc. No one has ever offered to help me. That might be kind of nice."

The Rescue Angels encapsulate it in light. I ask how the light feels.

"Well, not too bad."

"What did they tell you the Light would feel like?"

"Horrible, confining, burning, constricting, unpleasant. Make you so you couldn't breathe."

"Do you have a body?"

"No."

"I'm confused. If you don't have a body, what does it matter to you whether you can breathe or not?"

"That is a very, very good question. Why didn't I think of that? Well, I didn't have anywhere else to go."

"What else were you told about the Light?"

"There are bad things in the Light. Bad people in the Light."

"What would happen to you in the Light?"

"I'd disappear."

"Have you, with the light all around you, touching you?"

"No."

"Is the light burning? Go ahead, touch the light."

"It feels fine."

"What would you find if you looked deep inside?"

"Nothing, of course. Just like those other people."

"What did they discover?"

"Well! A spark! Wasn't that surprising!"

"I wonder if you have one of those. Go and look."

"I can't imagine that I do."

"Go. Drop right down to your center."

"I see a grain of a spark."

"You have one as well!"

"Oh, no!"

As it watches, the light grows. I ask how it feels. "Nice!"

At my invitation, it claims for the Light.

"The light is nice and I claim for the Light! So there, you other things!"

I ask if it would like to begin its recompense. "The sooner you begin, the sooner it's over?"

"It is. Are the few score that are left truly there?"

"They are. I thought you'd forget."

"Where are they now?"

"Every which way and hiding behind columns, being low, being skinny." I tell it to call them to the field. "They're scurrying. Oh, they mind so well!"

The Rescue Angels encapsulate them in light. At its instruction, they claim for the Light. Then, the ones at its level are called and reclaimed. Eleven levels above it are called and reclaimed before the one who sent it, The Evil One, is reached. It describes this one as "one stubborn one."

"He claims for the Light, but he is still not happy. He is CAUGHT!"

"He is not caught, he is freed. Show him how it feels to be free in the Light."

"He likes freedom."

As one last act of recompense, I tell the reclaimed one to describe to Laura how it and the few score that were left have affected her. "We've caused tension, strife, uneasiness, darkness, bleakness. Unhappiness, anger." I ask how else they have affected Laura. "Made her impatient. That was fun. Made her bite her nails when she was younger. She doesn't do that any more."

I ask Laura if she can forgive them. She does. They are taken to their place in the Light. The Rescue Angels and Healing Angels are called to do the gathering of the lost ones, the residue, and then the cleansing and healing of Laura.

Lineage: Bill's Story

I find in cases where an earthbound entity is in despair, a dark force entity is usually involved. The despair is a fine source of the energy the dark force entity looks to harvest, and even more desirable if the dark force entity has attached because of an agreement to link to the lineage of the human who so suffers. The agreement could have been made generations earlier, often as the first in the link is dying and offers the attachment in perpetuity as his part of a bargain to get something—a new body, power, etc.—from a dark force entity. Here is how this plays out for Bill's family:

When asked what it would say if it could speak, the tight, choking sensation in Bill's throat tries to avoid the question with, "Go away!" I discover that this is an earthbound entity that attached to Bill when he was eighteen. I ask how it was able to attach. It describes "feelings of unworthiness, guilt, shame, continual punishment of the self."

I ask for the name of the earthbound entity. This is Henry, Bill's father. Feelings of shame, helplessness, needing to get away, led Henry to hang himself in the barn. Henry tells me, "It was not the right thing to do." It was the eighteen-year-old Bill who found Henry's body.

The overwhelming sadness of the son and the father leads me to explore for the presence of a dark force entity.

There are five. I find them attached to Henry. They tell me they are now affecting Bill. The speaker for the five gives me another unexpected piece of information: they pass from one generation to the next through the father's line. Henry having died, they take Bill as next in line.

"There is no progress going on with Bill, and we are to attach to a male of the next generation. Since Bill has no male child, we are attempting to attach to his wife."

"Who gave you this assignment?"

"The one who hates the earthlings. One who cannot be named. Satan, from the Bible." I know from experience that it is highly unlikely for Satan to have gotten directly involved at this level. The dark force entity described as one who cannot be named would be farther down in the chain of command. I chalk this up as a scare tactic and am intrigued that they seem to follow biblical imagery, with "the one who cannot be named" presented as "Satan."

After the five and the dark force entities above them, all the way up to one who called itself Satan, are reclaimed, I offer the one who spoke for the five of them the opportunity to choose the name it will be known as in the Light. It chooses "Peter of the Light, a builder on the foundation of Light."

With this, the pact made with the darkness is dissolved, freeing Henry, Bill and all others in their line from the terms of the agreement—the forced harboring and influence of dark force entities. Henry is taken safely into the Light by the Rescue Angels and Bill no longer lives under the burden his ancestor created.

Truth-Telling

Before they are reclaimed, dark force entities are cagy, self-serving, very interested in admitting to as little as possible. They will do anything they can to harm and intimidate. And they lie.

Even after they have been given the opportunity to reexperience the Light they came from, often so very long ago, they are wary about giving up their survival skills. They tell half-truths about the harm they have done, to the extent of blaming it on "others" if they can. This is why they are pressed, as their final act of recompense (those acts providing them a direct benefit that they recognize and why they are willing to do them) to admit to everything they have done.

The point of this truth-telling is to provide the person victimized by the dark force entity a complete picture of what is the work of the dark force entity, and not an integral part of the client's life. As the order is expressed to the newly reclaimed dark force entity, "Tell them what is of you, and not them, and ceases immediately." It is a life-changing experience for the client.

Here are some of those truth-telling events given as that last act of recompense:

"I caused her to feel obligated, drained, caught, tethered. Thinking that is the way life had to be. I drained and tortured her."

"The burden of worrying about whether he is doing things correctly. The anxiety and fear and insecurity. I kept him from being hopeful and prevented him from seeing his own spark of light."

"Anger, rebellion, sadness, weakness, loneliness, ugliness."

"We keep her divided, keep energies from rising up from the solar plexus, keep power from flowing."

"I took up space, blocked his sight by sitting between him and his ability to see. The cause of the sadness he has felt."

"I was the gateway through which others entered."

"I squeezed her stomach to prevent her from discerning appropriate nourishment. Caused her to feel like rejecting the thing she needed most. Tried to prevent her from seeing the Light by shading her eyes so that she would see the dark blue (color) in her sleep. Poisoned her thoughts so that she would not feel that she would have the energy to accomplish her desires. Made her believe she was fatigued and did not want to get up and begin her day."

"We have continually warned her about the danger of being seen and the danger of having power as a woman. We have warned her not to use her power to assert herself when she is in the company of men, for we have convinced her that the men always have the true power. This will cease now. We have weakened her and brought confusion to her life plan, kept her from seeing clearly her path of greater joy. For we were always successful at laying down an undercurrent of fear to occlude her vision of joy. We have tried to keep her from speaking in public and we have tried to warn her to stay away from appearing in groups of people and being seen for her true power and beauty. We have made her afraid to be near others and to breathe on them. We have made her feel it is important to put up a shield to keep people at a distance."

"I gave her headaches so she would act like a pain. Lack of patience." I ask how the two dark entities it described as hiding "in the corners" affected her. "They made her very short-tempered, anxious."

"We were able to perpetuate the idea that he was always under threat. The safest thing was for him to project a menacing persona, such as having evil symbols around. We made his teeth crooked. This had been something we were actually proud of. Because we were positioned a little in front of him, we made people wary of him. They would sense that fear and withdraw from him."

"We caused him to look only to himself and not look outward to the needs and cares of others. We maintained that message of hate within and fed on the energy. We gave messages of all the things wrong and all the things that could go wrong, even in his dreams as he sleeps. We encouraged him to hate himself and his inability to find his way in his career and hate himself for not being a good father to his daughter as she was growing up. We influenced him to gamble and give up money and power. We were to bring him to a level so he would join us in trying to convince others to work in our mission of erasing the Light and the love of life."

The Archangels

I have observed that dark force entities do not work independently. All seem to be part of an organizational structure, with the one at the top of a pyramid controlling the focus and work of its underlings. Since the dark force entity at the top of the pyramid is very aware of its place in its system, Archangel Michael, who is at the top of his angelic pyramid, is called to be involved in that dark force entity's recovery.

What follows are some instances when we have been given more than the usual amount of information about these recoveries, some of it coming from the first dark force entity encountered after it had been recovered, and some from the angels.

Striking A Bargain

A dark force entity that has been returned to the light describes what happens when we are close to the top of its pyramid:

"There are two. They have spears and wings and smoke." They are encapsulated in light, then claim for the Light. The newly reclaimed dark force entity then calls the ones above these two to the field (an energy field of protection that was established by the Warrior Angels at the beginning of the session). One comes and is encapsulated in light. "It is looking around, trying to understand the transformation going on before it. And it is willing to claim for the Light. I tell you to claim for the Light! It seems to have created some dark structure around it. That action seems to have made some basic change in the structure surrounding the area. Like an earthquake."

We must be at the top of the pyramid, or very close. I tell this reclaimed dark force entity to call the one above it to the field. In its newly returned status, it may be willing to speak truthfully—if it is at the top of the pyramid, it will verify that it is, and if not, it will call in the one who rules this pyramid.

One more comes. I call on Archangel Michael and his workers to encapsulate it in light. Our commentator, the first reclaimed dark force entity, tells us the one at the top of its pyramid has black flapping wings and is the one causing the earth tremors.

The first reclaimed dark force entity tells the one at the top of the pyramid to claim for the Light. "There seems to be some recognition between Michael and this one. The recognition of having worked together in the past and the need this one feels for forgiveness before it can claim for the Light with any confidence. It is sending out big structures like black horns, like a black tree, making a lot of noise. Michael is quite amused."

I ask Michael if he will accept this one's request for forgiveness, on behalf of the Light. "Yes. He can be forgiven."

We are provided more commentary from the first dark force entity. "And that has caused the darkness and the vibrations to calm, and the structures to wilt and the giving up of the noise and the thunder and the need to swell up. There is rejoicing of Michael with this one. He seems to be willing to personally reeducate this one with love. And there is the forgiveness, and Michael is granting permission for some structure to be retained from the previous images. Michael is giving the message that all of the images can be accepted in the Light, and the most fundamental transformation in the Light will be the emotions, rather than the structures. That is a bargain that they have struck."

I ask our commentator what value this newly encapsulated one sees in the structures it has bargained with Michael to keep. "Michael knows that this is a childish request, but it will be a part of this one's education to learn that the structures that gave it power and that it used to intimidate can be transformed into light and will no longer be used for swelled-up intimidation."

I will be seeing more of this one, whom Michael has taken on to educate, in my future work.

Gabriel, Michael And Friend

In a later session when we again encounter a dark force entity, it agrees to call the members of its pyramid to the protective field established for us by the Warrior Angels. The last two the restored dark force entity calls appear to have claws. When they claim for the Light, the restored dark force entity observes, "They have given up their claws."

I expect there to be one more yet to call, and the restored dark force entity tells me, "There are no more at this point. I can see two angels surrounding the last two that came and, in the middle, there is a white angel with wings spread like a dove." I ask what the angel is called. "Gabriel, for he is a teacher. And Michael is on the left and on the right is someone in violet robes." I ask for that one's name. "A-z-u-i-l, maybe." I ask if they are all archangels. "Yes."

I ask Gabriel how it is that he has come to do this work. "This is work where we have gathered a hierarchy that reaches down to the earth plane and touches many through their devotion to witchcraft. We are here to teach all of this hierarchy and to reach all of the individuals on the earth plane who have been touched by these lower forces. For by targeting the individuals on the earth plane through this hierarchy, we can identify souls who feel lost and disoriented. As we project our light down to this hierarchy, we can touch the roots of evil and fill these souls who continue to exist on the earth plane with light. For they were looking for the Light, and, because of their lack of education, and because of their vulnerability and their adolescent years, they were experimenting with choices that led them to dark force entities. So, by replacing each connection that formerly was held by a dark force energy with the golden light of truth, we can have a great effect on the earth plane, on each of these souls that is asking for help. Because the dark force has been removed from the aura of each soul, we are able to shower the soul with light."

I thank Gabriel and ask Azuil what his contribution is to this work. "I am assisting Michael in his work, and I am in training with Michael to be a Captain of the Warrior Angels and to learn techniques at this level that I can teach to the Warrior Angels, for I recognize that many of the ones that we have in this pyramid will need to go on, or elect to go on, and work as Warrior Angels." I ask Azuil if he is referring to the ones who have now chosen the Light. "Yes."

The reference to being in training with Archangel Michael makes me wonder if Azuil is the same one Archangel Michael offered to educate in that earlier session.

I am unwilling to accept the possibility that we have reached the top of this pyramid, even though the recovered dark force entity seems to have moved beyond the need for subterfuge. I turn to Archangel Michael and ask if there are those above these two with claws that continue this chain upward. "No." I ask if this chain is complete. "Yes. It was a very large chain with a very large footprint on the earth. A very large pyramid with a great base." I ask if we have missed any along the pyramid. "There is still work for you,

Maureen. This pyramid is complete. There are others. This is a huge pyramid that is complete. It had techniques for learning how to entice young souls." O.K. then. I quit with my questions, feeling a little sheepish for checking up on Archangel Michael to make sure he is doing his job.

I would like to state that I am not claiming that those who practice Wicca, those who refer to themselves as white witches and work with and in support of the earth's energies, are involved in the witchcraft described here.

The One In Violet Robes

Some time later, when I again have the opportunity to ask Michael questions, I get my curiosity about that angel in violet satisfied. I ask Michael, "Is the one who appeared to be in violet robes, the one that had been reclaimed, the same as the one who recognized you and you him? The one who wanted to take its structure with it into the Light?"

Michael's response: "Yes. One that had been with me, struck out on his own and eventually learned through your work that the only power is love, and only through light will he be able to continue on. Without the Light, there is continuous confusion and searching and attempts to overpower other beings and other consciousnesses, but no true success or expansion. There is no ability to create anything new. There is only the ability to copy or replicate what already exists."

I ask one last question: "Have we spelled this one's name correctly?" Michael obliges, responding to that earlier confusion I had with the angel's name, and replies, "A-z-i-e-l." Now we have another angel to call on: a Captain of the Warrior Angels, Aziel of the Light.

Aziel Of The Light

Aziel and I now work together. He is my eyes when I want to know if a client has been cleared of attached entities. He confirms that an entity has crossed the threshold into the Light. Most importantly, Aziel works with the dark force entities in the higher levels of a pyramid, just as Archangel Michael did for him, to help them choose for the Light.

Other Pyramids

I have had opportunities to ask Archangel Michael about the focus of two other dark force entity pyramids.

The first pyramid: "Communication and the media. Feeding thoughts of fear and destruction by repeating the most gruesome stories and bringing down those who read the newspaper or watch the repetition of disasters over and over on television."

The second pyramid: "It was involved in capturing terror and distributing the love of terror in the culture, trying to attract young people to the media of terror and to establish as a norm for the society the seeking of terror as entertainment. The absence of light and the interference of the patterns of light, making terror a reality, rather than an illusion. Although the pyramid has been removed, the memory will remain in the minds of people. It will take longer to die out. People will continue believing that it is a true form of entertainment to offer terrorizing experiences to the young. Therefore, send greater harmony and light into the studios where videos are made—to create a gradual change so that society will not notice. It will feel like a withdrawal if the change occurs too suddenly."

With this, we, all of us who care about the well-being of humanity, have been given a vital task to perform.

Making Deals With The Devil

Dark force entities are ever on the hunt for new recruits. They prey on weakness, fear, greed. The ones among their members who have successfully been reunited with the Light have told of being tricked, as they expressed it, into becoming a part of the dark community. An offer is made, they accept, and the deal is sealed.

The offer is always a lure of some kind, a promise given to fill a desire. A promise that is either empty, or for something that is already within the capacity of their victim.

Once the deal is made, the victims are held hostage by threats of pain and destruction. And then the work of the victims begins. They are given tasks to perform to produce the energy the dark ones thrive on.

Above all else, the victims are fed the illusion that they are not free to make choices to save themselves. No choice to refuse the assignment, no choice to dissolve the pact. Hidden from them is the truth that the servitude can all be ended with a simple declaration: "I choose for the Light."

The dark force entities are opportunistic feeders. It is not only souls they target. They are willing to take still embodied humans, if they can get them. And get them they do.

In every instance where an individual, whether human or earthbound entity, is found to be bound under an agreement made with a dark force entity, both the victim and the dark force entity are restored to the Light.

As the focus in this chapter is on the ones who are enslaved, the work done to reunite the involved dark force entities with the Light may not be referenced.

Jessie

I recall how terrified Jessie's mother, Alicia, seemed when I first met the family. I had been invited to their home in hopes that I could do something about the unaccountable noises her girls had been hearing in the bedroom at night.

We sat around the kitchen table, I listening to their stories before I began the clearing work. In the midst of the back and forth, Alicia asked her fifteen-year-old, Jessie, to talk about the voice she had been hearing. I looked at Alicia, knowing what this could mean. Alicia did too.

The voice had been whispering to Jessie, offering her wonderful powers. All she had to do was kill her stepbrother, and it knew she wanted to do it.

Jessie was terrified by the voice, the offer, the attraction she felt to do the deed. She clutched the cross she wore around her neck and prayed every time the voice returned. It would not leave.

We scheduled a session for Jessie for the next day. She would continue with her temporary solution until we met. I did the space clearing for the family before I left.

We discovered the dark force entity seated in an empty space around Jessie's heart, making those promises and amplifying the discord between Jessie and her stepbrother. The only thing keeping it from the final step of possession was her refusal to accept its offer.

We did the work to reunite the dark force entity with the community of Light and free Jessie of its influence. Then there was more work to be done for her. Jason, the earthbound entity we also found attached to Jessie, was released and helped to complete his transition into the Light. Jason's story is in the chapter, Suicide.

A lighter, brighter, beautiful girl left my office. She was unaware how close a call it had been. I, for my part, was relieved that her life had been given back to her.

Ambrose

Life ends for Ambrose, the dancer, in 1415 or 1416, he can't exactly recall. He tells me, "What difference does it make! I had toes and a nose and now I don't have them!"

Ambrose has caused so much havoc for Andrea that I am convinced his story of having "tippy toes and a nose" is just another instance of a dark force entity hiding behind a facade. As it turns out, we discover that a dark force entity is using Ambrose's passionate desire to be back on his dancing toes as a bargaining chip. The dark force entity explains, "In order for me to get you to do what I wanted you to do, you really wanted to have tippy toes and a nose, so I told you you had them and, if you would stay here, you would keep your tippy toes and nose. No one else thought it, but you thought you had them."

Ambrose finally understands that it is not that he has lost track of his beloved tippy toes—his body has failed and his toes and nose are no more. He agrees to be taken into the Light. With the promise of another body and another time to dance.

The dark force entity is helped to reclaim the Light and is delivered to its place in the Light, Ambrose says his good-byes to Andrea and is carried across the threshold into the Light by the Rescue Angels, and Andrea is free of both of them.

Horace

The entity we discover attached to Olivia shares vivid memories of a volcano with us, then gives a detailed description of a ship's portal. The memories, disjointed as they are, strike me as having a sense of reality. I am guessing this entity is an earthbound drawing on its memories of a life lived in a body even though it has little recall of that time. By the end of Olivia's session, we have the whole story.

I begin by asking how it attached to Olivia. It describes coming in through an open portal. "I walked right in. I waltzed in." It describes the portal as round, like a portal in a ship with glass that you can see through.

The open portal in Olivia has me concerned. We do not come equipped with open portals. A dark force entity has been at work. And I doubt that this earthbound merely happened upon the opening in Olivia's energy.

I ask the entity who it is who is talking. "Horace." Our "it" has a human name and thinks of itself as a "he." More indication that this soul is human. I want to make sure. I ask Horace what he thinks he would find if he were to look inside himself. He tells me he expects to find "Nothing worthwhile. Nothing worth looking for. Nothing."

Another hint that Horace's attachment to Olivia was not his own idea. Some outside influence has convinced Horace that he is empty inside. Moreover, he has been encouraged to avoid checking to see what he might find.

He takes me up on my suggestion that he check for himself.

"Boy! There's a lot of light in here! It's blinding!" I ask who the light belongs to. "Well, they told me it couldn't belong to me." I ask if it feels familiar. "I don't quite know it, but it feels familiar. I haven't seen it for quite some time." I ask how long. "Eons and eons."

Though I am interested in the "they" who tried to direct Horace away from the Light, there is other business to attend to first if we are to help him out of the fix I suspect he is in.

I ask Horace if he can recall the last time he saw the light inside himself. I get a cryptic "I died" in response. He is beginning to remember the life he lost. I ask Horace if he had a body. "I think I had a body. I don't see a body around, but I think I had one."

I ask who gave him the name Horace. "Them." I ask what year it is for him. "1166." I ask who the "them" are that gave him this name. "I want to say Vikings, but I can't imagine that that is true." I can.

When I suggest that he skip back to the last time he was in his body, Horace recalls, "Sea. Air. Wind. Water." He is about eleven.

He remembers a great big crashing and he ends up in the water. Sees "lots of green and blue. Gurgling and bubbles. That's it."

Horace sees his body floating away. He floats in one direction, his body in another. He finds himself floating around in a mass of cold, green, weird water. The perspective of one still young enough to see the world through curious eyes.

"They find me and tell me that I could get out of the mass of green swirling water and they would send me to a different place. Which they did, and it was away from green swirling water." And right into Olivia, I am thinking.

The "them" who named Horace had to have been his family. The "they" who promised to get Horace out of the water are far from the same. This looks suspiciously like the work of dark force entities snagging a newly dead, confused young boy.

I ask Horace what he had to do in order to be sent out of the green swirling water. "I had to recruit more people or things or beings or whatever. I had to recruit. I did a lot of recruiting." I ask if the ones he found to recruit were floating around like he was. "Um-hum, yeah. I gathered them up and shoved them, pushed them toward portals. Slipped them in."

And what was Horace to get for this? "Out of the cold swirling water. And I was to get a body. So I've been living here for a while."

I ask if there is someone already in the body he is in. "Of course!"

"And not you?"

"Right. I'm just here."

Just to make sure Horace understands he is not only dead, but bodiless, I tell him he doesn't have a body, like they promised, because this body belongs to Olivia, and not him.

I ask Horace if he has had enough of their lies and would like our help. He agrees. He repeats the Renunciation of the Darkness (see Appendix 2) after me and claims for the Light. Horace finds the light "relieving."

It is time to get Horace home. I tell him that there are those who wait for him in the Light. Horace says he can hear them calling now. His friends. He doesn't see them, but can hear them.

Before he is taken into the Light, he tells Olivia, "I'm sorry I've caused you havoc." I ask Horace to tell her what was his doing, and not a part of her. "It was endless! Lost things, disappearing, out of sight, gone mysteriously." Then, "I was working in the wings and some of the things I did, others did as well. I just kind of helped a lot. Made her feel cold." An explanation about as disjointed as the volcano/portal descriptions Horace gave us when we first found him. It will do. Olivia now knows she is free.

Looking For Glory

Fred was a toddler, just beginning to walk, when the entity found him. He had been on the ground, crying, his knees scraped and wanting someone to come pick him up and comfort him.

The entity had no interest in giving Fred the comfort he so longed for. This was far from a random attachment—the entity tells us it was sent by "someone who carries a hook, someone who rips flesh." Its job was to gather blood to feed to "the others." When I ask what would happen to it if it failed at its job, it tells me it is afraid that its skin would rip.

I wonder what kind of blood this one has been collecting. Clearly it is impossible for it to be physically letting Fred's blood. I ask the entity what it has done to Fred. Not collecting blood, I discover. It prodded Fred to behavior that could be milked for the energy "the others" feed on. It made Fred aggressive, "not to be left alone" for fear of the damage Fred would do. Fred goes from a sad little boy looking for comfort to an unlikeable fellow who has to be constantly watched. He is now in his fifties. Life has not been easy for him.

This skin-ripping business might be an illusion produced to cow a bodiless dark force entity into compliance by its controllers. I need to be clear about what we have encountered. I ask if the entity recalls having a body of its own.

It remembers having one in 1720. Being promised "glory" if it would do this work. Not a dark force entity. An earthbound caught in the grips of the dark ones' influence.

When I ask this earthbound if it is aware of the current year, to my surprise it hits it right on the nose. It is more common for an earthbound to be aware only of the year of its death.

I make use of the little gift that is handed to me. This is the doorway I can use to help the earthbound see how completely it has been fooled. Out loud, I make the observation that years have passed since that promise was made. It may be obvious to me. It is a new thought to the earthbound. It now is painfully aware that it has been waiting a very, very long time for its reward.

I offer a way out of the agreement made centuries ago. The earthbound willingly breaks its pact with the dark force entity. Its first act as a freed soul is to claim for the Light that was there for it all along. Fred is free now as well. The goading stops, and with it the dark influence that added to his lifelong depression.

Satsuma

Satsuma is a cagy earthbound who doesn't give up her identity easily. She gives hazy answers to my questions. Maybe she is from "an old year, I don't think zero," or maybe she has forgotten. Maybe her name is really Liz, or her name could have been taken away from her. Which she doesn't mind because she likes the sound of Satsuma better. She knows she had a body even though it's been gone for "quite some time." She remembers last being in it at age thirty.

After a great deal of talk I get to the bottom of things with Satsuma. She attached to Hope, a sweet girl of six or ten (specifics aren't Satsuma's strong suit) and is hanging out with Hope because, Satsuma explains, she has gotten "lost, really lost."

Satsuma seems to understand that she is not the owner of this particular body, even though she feels like she hasn't been in the way—she is light as a feather and, besides, Hope doesn't know she's there. Sheesh!

I decide it's time to give Satsuma a nudge in the right direction and ask her if she would like a body of her own. All the coyness evaporates. "Yeah, sure! I've heard that before!" I ask who has told her this. "Those others. Those soldier, standup types. I don't know if they're soldiers or not, but they stand straight. And wooden-like. They told me I was going to get a body. I have not gotten a body!"

I suspect some deal making has gone on. I ask if they told Satsuma she had to do something for them to get a body. "Well, maybe."

I point out that she doesn't have to do anything for them or anyone else, only to choose to have another body.

The caginess reappears. "Of my own? Not someone else's that I'm just looking after, right?" I ask if she has done that before. "Oh, I've done that before." I ask what happened to the other bodies she was attached to. "I don't know what happened to them." I ask if they died. "Definitely. That's what happened."

I decide to do some bargaining myself and ask Satsuma if she is getting a little tired of not having her own way of doing things. If she would like us to help her with that. "The obvious answer is yes."

Satsuma wants to know how much it is going to cost her. This one must have some experience with how to go about getting the best out of a negotiation. I say it will not cost her, as it is her right.

"My right?" I tell her it is her right to choose. She just hasn't done that. "Well, no one has offered it. I didn't know it was an option! It won't be the original one, will it? I don't think I liked the original one." I ask what it was like. "Ugly comes to mind. Maybe deformed. I think I was very short. Maybe on-my-knees short. I didn't like it. It was not a good body." Satsuma is looking for an upgrade. She wants a fully functioning, Class A body.

I again make the offer to help. This time she takes me up on it. I suggest she look way, way up. "I see lightness." I urge her to look further up and she sees a little gray, then looks higher. "It's kind of like flying." I ask her to stay with us and just look. "I see lightness." She is reluctant to look into the Light, afraid that it will burn. More misinformation from the dealmakers.

I want to hear this from her and ask who has told her this. "The Other One." Typical of the type of names assigned to dark force entities by the ones they control. I tell her first of all, The Other One was lying, and we aren't asking her to get close to the Light, just to look into it.

When she does, she observes once again that the Light has lightness, as in nonheavy. Satsuma is beginning to be aware of the difference between the density of the earth and the significantly finer energy of the Light. She is doing more exploring and less bargaining. A very good sign.

I ask her if she can see the one who is waiting for her. "I see a hand stretched out, but no face." I suggest she touch the hand with one finger. "It feels warm." I ask her to look for the face. "I don't see a face, but I'd like to think that it is kindly."

I ask if she would like to be with that one. "Yes, as long as it doesn't extract from me something I have to do. Everyone else has wanted something. I tried to turn them down."

And so we have come to the real reason Satsuma hasn't been able to leave. I ask if she made them any promises. "Oh, scores of promises. I think I'd prefer not to remember. They were not good promises."

I ask what she would get if she did things for them. "That they would leave me alone, wouldn't throw me in the pit, and that I could stay in this body. And wouldn't have to move again."

I tell her they promised her things they couldn't give. "Well, I've stayed in the body."

"Yes, but that is because you chose to do so, not that they could offer you that."

"That's a horse of a different color, isn't it?"

I make the comment that she made some promises that have created a problem for her. "Yes, but I tried to renege on them."

I ask if she would like to clear them up. "I want to wipe the slate clean." She repeats the Renunciation of the Darkness after me.

When the dissolution of the contract is completed, one that Satsuma tells us she made centuries ago, I ask Satsuma how she feels. "Kind of lonesome, like I don't know where I'm going. I have nothing around me, just me!"

I once again suggest she look up into the Light. She sees more than one face. One is vaguely familiar to her as it has been a long time since she has seen it. I tell Satsuma to watch as that one steps forward, and I ask her who it is. "Marda. She left me behind." Skeptical, Satsuma asks, "Is it true or something else?" I suggest she look in Marda's eyes.

"All the eyes I have been looking at recently have been red. I don't want them to be red!" For good reason. Dark force entities can create a convincing illusion of being human, with the exception of the eyes. They are always red. In case the faces Satsuma sees are dark force entities masquerading as humans Satsuma has known, I call on the Rescue Angels to gather up all imposters and carry them to their place in the Light.

Satsuma then sees someone with brown eyes. It is not Marda, and is not someone she recognizes. The eyes feel okay, she just doesn't know them. She tells us she is being cautious. "It is very scary! I don't want to go from the pot to the fire."

I encourage her to touch this one's hand with her finger. "It doesn't feel hot or cold, just kind of tepid." I ask if she likes the way it feels. She does. I ask if she would like to be with this one, and others waiting for her as well.

"Forever?"

"What does forever mean for you, Satsuma?"

"Centuries and centuries."

Satsuma's experience of time on earth. I decide to let her discover for herself what it is to be beyond time. Then I reassure her that this one does not have a body that will go away and leave her behind. She agrees to be taken to them.

Before she leaves, Satsuma tells Hope, "I'm sorry I made you tired all the time, nonproductive. And to procrastinate, too. That was my main job." I affirm that Satsuma's influence on Hope ends immediately. Satsuma tells us, "I'm very relieved that I don't have to do that any more!"

A real change of heart from the tough little haggler who wanted us to believe she was light as a feather and not at all in the way. Hope forgives her. The Rescue Angels lift Satsuma into the Light.

Shin

When Kim scans her body, she describes her left foot as white hot and trying not to be noticed. It might as well have been wearing a sign reading, "Look here first!"

I offer whatever it is that hides in Kim's foot a chance to speak. There is another attempt to deflect. "You are stupid to look here." More like, "You got me!" When I probe to verify that this is something other than Kim, the response is, "We are someone else." Six of them, it says.

The one that has been doing the talking orders one of the others to speak, warning it that it will be switched with a bamboo switch. A threat that it is not to give up their identity. It promptly does.

It tells me there are three of them who have been alive in physical human bodies. Six others, attempting to paint themselves white, have not. These six miss that there is an obvious difference between covering themselves with white and being light. This is not the first time I have encountered this subterfuge. Altogether, then, there are nine. Three earthbound entities and six that are most likely dark force entities.

I continue the conversation with the switched one. It gives its name as Shin. He recalls being alive in 1460. He was a Japanese warrior, proudly equipped with armor and sword.

Shin goes into battle, "looking for glory." The glory he had been promised. It did not come. He was struck down in battle before he could engage. A great shame for a warrior such as he.

I ask Shin who it was that had promised him the glory to be claimed on a battlefield. "Others, not the Emperor."

There were four, plus two leaders. The six "others" who painted themselves white when we discovered them have finally been exposed, as I suspected, for their true selves: dark force entities.

Shin tells us that when they first made him that promise of glory, they appeared to be war gods. Shin, looking at the one who made the pact with him, sees it shrinking, now suddenly a weak, frightened, tattered beggar with a rat at its side. Hardly able to bear being looked upon.

This is a real eye opener for Shin. He says in disgust, "The war gods we believed were fools!" Immediately, he abandons his allegiance to them. He tells us, "I see I have true choices now, rather than shackles and the switch."

I help Shin reconstruct what happened to him when his life ended. He recalls that when they died, he and his comrades stayed with the swords and armor they had worn into battle. Eventually their war gear, with them still attached, became part of a display in the museum in New York visited by Kim and her mother when Kim was very young. She, feeling confused and lost, knowing only that her mother had taken her away to escape Kim's father.

Attaching to Kim was Shin's assignment. He was to keep her in fear of moving forward. Afraid of any movement at all.

There is just one step left to complete Shin's liberation. I ask him to look above him and tell me what he notices.

When Shin looks up, the clouds part and he sees a bright light. In the light is a woman and children. Shin recognizes his mother and his small sister. Waiting for him in the Light.

As a parting gift, Shin tells Kim, "She is strong and life is not a battle. She can flow through life."

I turn my attention to the beggar and its rat, trying to slink away. Humans do not shapeshift. This and the fact that it pushed Shin out in front at the beginning of the encounter have dark force entity written all over it. And always dark force entities have an assignment.

It boasts of being given a job of high importance. It was to gather souls from the battlefield. Shin must have been one among many.

When the Rescue Angels encapsulate this dark force entity in light, it treats Kim to a rare experience of its transformation. "I see tiny seeds of brilliant blue light that join with the light of the capsule. I feel complete. The waves and photons of light are then completing the structure of light that had been absent."

Dark force entities have so lost themselves in the darkness they no longer know their own names. I want to mark this one's return to the Light Community. I offer it an opportunity to name itself. It chooses to be called Jacob, as the name has a familiarity to it, from reading. I suppose over Kim's shoulder.

Jacob makes recompense for the damage it has caused Kim by admitting to how it has affected her, both so it accepts responsibility and so Kim will know that the damage it has caused ends now. "I have made her wary of having to engage in battle on a regular basis. Battles are an illusion. When the photons and the waves of light are united, there is harmony." Stunning for that to be coming from one who had been so committed to destruction.

I have not forgotten about that rat. Dark force entities' only interest is in self-preservation. I saw no possibility that the "beggar" would have a rat as a little buddy—as if a beggar can't afford to have a real pet, so a rat will do. If I could look past the terrible things they had done, I could almost see the charm in the disguise.

Predictably, the rat is another dark force entity. When this one is reestablished in the Light, it chooses the name Roland. Because "I have seen one of that name who has admirable strength and light."

There is a bit of the poetic in Roland's description of his influence over Kim: "I made her feel inadequate to the tasks at hand, and experience self-doubt that need not be present. Her true glory and completeness can shine through now."

The Controller

When an earthbound is discovered hiding out in Carol, it shouts out, "Run away!" Fearful. The light it comes from is "a vermilion-red color." Not dark, not the white light of lost human souls. The color of blood.

My initial impression that this earthbound is terrified is confirmed as the questioning continues. It is afraid to tell me the kinds of things that attached earthbounds usually find nonthreatening: when it attached, how it affects Carol, where it was the last time it was in its own body. All of this because it fears if it tells me, I will have power over it, and if someone has power over it, that one can take it away from its work. It seems to be consumed by this fear of losing its "work." It cannot recall the year it had last been in its body because that is being hidden so it will focus on its work. If it tells what work it does, its work will be a failure and it will be beaten.

Being beaten is a personal thing. Very different from vague statements about work and failure. We're finally having a conversation. I ask who will beat it. Something called The Controller, who sent it to Carol.

I ask if The Controller is watching. Often they are.

"Yes."

The Controller will most likely engage with me, since I am treading on its territory. I begin with the usual, asking if it has a memory of having a body, and the color of the light in its original place, expecting to find a dark force entity behind the terrorizing.

It has been human. Its light is "billowing clouds of grey and black." You just never know.

I ask who has sent it and it blusters, "*I* am in charge." By way of explanation, it tells me it has to be in charge to keep the ones below it in line. I ask how many it has under it.

"Twenty or thirty."

If there are ones below it, inevitably there is someone or something over it. I ask if this is the case. "I dare not look on his face." And what would happen if it did? "The darkness would descend and engulf me." Has it tried? (And I would be surprised if it has.) "No. I know the rules."

So we have a rule maker, most likely not a human, even though the earthbound, who has called itself The Controller, refers to it as being male. Is the one who made the rules also the one who would cause darkness to descend? The reply, "Yes." And is it watching? "Yes." Good. We can talk.

I ask the one who made the rules if it had a body of its own. "No. Therefore I am untouchable by one such as you." Arrogant, hostile. Ah, but communicating with me. I discover the answers to the questions the first earthbound feared to give. The Controller sent the first earthbound to Carol at age eight years, eight months. An odd answer. Still, we now know the interference has been going on since childhood. This will be helpful for Carol to know.

Carol's loneliness was its gateway. The dark force entity describes the assignment: "to funnel the energy up, keep her from moving forward and prevent her from feeling alive and to prevent her from going out in the world and doing work in the Light."

We have a long conversation regarding how successful they have been with the work and what is going to happen to it since it admits it has not been successful.

I am given a colorful description of the threat the one who made the rules lives under: "My wings will be burnt and my power will be taken away."

We do the work to help this one reconnect with the Light.

Once this dark force entity's influence is cleared, I turn to the first earthbound, the one so fearful of being discovered. I am hoping it will be willing to accept help.

This time when I ask, he remembers being alive. Throbbing pain, unable to breathe and pressed down into the earth by stomping feet. Then the pact he makes.

Trying to weasel out of responsibility for what he has done, the first earthbound claims Carol permitted him to stay. I am not buying this. I tell him firmly that she did not and that he has overstepped his bounds by inhabiting a body that is not his.

I ask what he was to get out of the deal he made. They promised that he would continue to live and they would keep him alive even though his body was broken. For his part, he was to do work for them. He was to help them gather others for their army, their minions.

Again, denying his culpability, the first earthbound says he tried to do the work, but did not gather any souls. Had very little influence on others. I am not buying this, either. I point out that he made the agreement and did their work. Oh, no. He only tried to do their work and since he failed it should not count against him. This does not even come close to the story he started with. He is so wrapped up in self-preservation he is not going to be capable of making the first move to free himself.

He will, though, probably understand he made a bad deal. I tell him they promised something that was not theirs to give. They had no bodies to hand out. If he had wanted a body of his own, all he had to do was choose for himself. This he gets. "They lied to me!" I ask him to revoke the contract. He agrees. He repeats the Renunciation of the Darkness after me. Now he is on his way.

When he looks into the Light, he sees members of his village reaching out, beckoning him to come to them. One steps forward, his brother. This will be the one to reconnect him to the Light. His brother's eyes "feel like love." His hand feels "refreshing and inviting and filled with love," confirming for us that the path has been cleared.

Before he is taken to the Light, he apologizes to Carol for attaching to her and trying to extract her life force for himself. Honesty, humility. A soul returned. Carol grants him forgiveness. He is carried into the Light.

I turn to the second earthbound, the one labeled The Controller, inviting him to remember who he had been. The memories come flooding back. He recalls being with pirates and wind, and water flowing over him. The water goes into his nose and throat. He struggles and dies.

He admits to me that he made a pact with the dark ones before he died. They promised him power and control, with many under him. To be a captain of many. Bitterly, he tells us he was made a captain of many, but they did not function. They had no bodies, no capacity to do the things he assumed they would be able to do.

When The Controller made his pact with the darkness, he envisioned taking over whole fleets of ships and becoming wealthy. A man with abundant possessions.

The bargain he struck was familiar to one who had been a privateer such as he. In return for being made captain, he agreed to share everything that he could acquire and pass it upward. Too late he discovered how uneven this deal would be. They had made a promise, in his words, "but it was empty." They certainly took energy from him, and what he got in return was a sham.

He wants out of this. He repeats the Renunciation of the Darkness after me.

His world shifts. He finds himself feeling free and expansive and has more power than he ever felt before. It is, I tell him, the power of the Light. I can almost feel his recognition.

The best is yet to come. When he looks up into the Light, he sees his childhood playmates. He sees his mother and father in the background. His mother steps forward. When he looks into her eyes they are green, her natural color. Intensely loving. When he touches her hand, he says, "It feels like coming home."

In these last minutes we spend with The Controller, who was not able to recall his name, long forgotten as was his mother's love, the man he had once been comes back into focus. Honest in his own way. Able to lead and stay the course. The Controller's parting words to Carol, "I am sorry we attempted to drain your energy. And I ask forgiveness." We send him on his way with our blessing.

Part 5: The Way Forward

The Way Forward

My intention in writing *Clearings* is first to shine light on the source of unrecognized influences so that interference ceases and healing can be realized. Secondly, it is to lift out of the realm of fear all those who have fallen prey to fear's seductive influence.

If we view those souls who have gotten off course at the completion of their time on earth with compassion rather than with fear or as a source of entertainment, we open the door to freeing ourselves from the burden of an attachment and liberating the ones who could spend centuries wandering before they find the way home.

If we can recognize those who have become entrapped by the influence of the darkness as the lost souls they truly are, we can offer them the way back to light.

Lastly, my intention is to share with my readers how interconnected is the world in which we live. And how love is the glue that holds us all together.

Acknowledgements

Heartfelt thanks to Christine Deignan, Sydney Maresca and Virginia Reyna for time generously given, invaluable insight, and asking me for more when I thought that more wasn't there. Thanks also to Paulus Zegwaard for keeping the ship afloat, and most of all, for believing.

Appendices

Appendix 1: The Sealing Light Meditation

The Reverend Judith Baldwin, developer of the Baldwin Method of Spirit Releasement with William J. Baldwin, Ph.D., wrote this visualization as a way to build protection for clients coming for spirit releasement therapy.

The visualization is an easy, effective way to create a calming space when day-to-day life becomes frantic. This is the long version. Once you have used it a few times, it can take just a few seconds to set up the protective energy bubble for yourself.

Sealing Light Meditation

Imagine now, begin to visualize, deep within your chest, a brilliant point of light. It is your connection with the Light, your connection to Source. See this light expand all throughout your body, feel the energy flow from the top of your head to the tips of your toes, across your shoulders, down your arms to your fingertips. Imagine that the light is expanding out past the boundaries of your body, outside your physical form, an arm's length in every direction: in front of you, behind you, on either side of you, above your head and down beneath your feet. See and feel this light lovingly, protectingly, surrounding you like a large egg-shaped bubble of light. Begin to imagine, sparkling through the bubble of light, bits of emerald green, the color of the energy of healing, and bits of rose pink, the color of the energy of love. Every cell of your body has its own intelligence and will use this healing energy for the highest good of the entire organism. This cocoon of light does not interfere with the expression of love, as you love others, or the experience of love, as others love you. Take another deep breath of light and begin to come back into your body. Completely back into your body. Reconnect your consciousness with every cell of your physical body. Take control, take charge of your own body. When you are ready to open your eyes into your own regular state of consciousness, you can do that. Another deep breath of light now, and come back.

Take a few moments several times a day for the next few weeks and repeat this meditation to yourself. Repeat this meditation when you awaken and before you go to sleep. Take a few seconds every time you feel tired or unhappy. Do it every time you feel happy and when you smile. See and feel this light every time you breathe. Soon it will be with you permanently. This is your continued protection.

Appendix 2: Renunciation Of The Darkness

The chapter, Making Deals With The Devil, contains accounts of earthbound entities who made agreements with dark force entities. Once such a contract is made, it is necessary to end it with a declaration in order for the earthbound entity to be freed. The client speaks the Renunciation of the Darkness on behalf of the earthbound entity.

William J. Baldwin, Ph.D., and the Reverend Judith Baldwin have written the following Renunciation of the Darkness for that purpose.

In instances when clients have made a pact with the darkness, the contracts can be dissolved by their repeating the Renunciation of the Darkness for themselves.

Renunciation Of The Darkness

In the name of the Light, I rebuke you, darkness.
I renounce all activities of the darkness.
I revoke all contracts and agreements,
rituals and initiations,
invitations and acceptances,
invocations and summonings,
pacts and bargains,
with and from and to the darkness.
I refuse and reject all promises and gifts, glamours, powers and seductions,
with and to and from the darkness.

Throughout eternity, for as long as my soul exists.
For in the name of the Light, it is so.

Appendix 3: Indicators Of An Attachment

The myriad ways an attachment can occur point to the possibility that many people are living with the influence of an attached entity. Some of the indicators that this is the case include:

- A feeling of heaviness, as if one is carrying an extra weight
- Hearing voices in your head
- Emotional outbursts, especially anger
- Difficulty sleeping
- Difficulty concentrating
- A sudden mood change, such as becoming depressed or anxious
- Abusive use of mind-altering drugs, including alcohol
- Surviving a traumatic event
- Not feeling like yourself after a hospital stay for an illness or surgery
- Experimentation with *séances*, satanic rituals
- Discomfort with information regarding entity attachment
- Experiencing urges to carry out destructive acts

Glossary

Archangel Gabriel

Archangel Gabriel describes his specialty as teacher in the chapter, Prisoners Of Darkness.

Archangel Michael

Archangel Michael is the leader of the angels who defend the Light. He is often seen as a protector as well. In spirit releasement work, Michael is the angel who is called on to encapsulate dark force entities at the higher levels of the dark force entities' chains of command and to escort these entities to their place in the Light. The Warrior Angels and the Rescue Angels work under Archangel Michael's direction.

Archangels

Angels, beings of light who do not take on an earth life, can be categorized into a hierarchy based on their form of service. Archangel is the highest level of angel working to assist humanity. Each archangel has a specialty, and assigns tasks to the angels who work under the archangel's direction.

Aziel Of The Light, A Captain Of The Warrior Angels

Aziel's story can be found in the chapter, Prisoners Of Darkness. Thought at first to have the name Azuil, Aziel is what might be described as a fallen angel. With Archangel Michael's assistance, Aziel reclaimed for the Light. His new job as a member of Archangel Michael's forces is to be in training as a Captain of the Warrior Angels, working to rescue other dark force entities and return them to the Light.

Chi

Chi is a term used to describe the life force energy contained in all living beings.

Dark Force Entities

Dark force entities are beings of the light communities under the control of the darkness. They may also be referred to as fallen angels. At some point in their history, these angels make a pact with the leaders of the dark force entities to be under their control. They carry out the work of the darkness under the threat of punishment. There is a sort of chain of command, with each level controlling the level below it. Moving up in the ranks occurs after a dark force entity suffers punishment for failing at its assigned task. See the chapters, Prisoners Of Darkness and Making Deals With The Devil.

Earthbound Entities/Earthbounds

Earthbound entities are beings on earth who have separated from their bodies at death and then, instead of completing the death process and returning to the Light, stay close to the earth. For a fuller description, see the chapter, Becoming Earthbound.

Earthbounds And Humans Controlled By Dark Force Entities

Humans who, at the time of their deaths, resist being drawn into the Light, are presented with an offer from a dark force entity to "improve" their situation. If they accept the offer they must pledge to work for the dark in exchange for help. They are caught in servitude, often assigned to attach to a human and thus create destruction for their human host. The chapter, Making Deals With The Devil, tells their stories.

Humans, fully alive, will also be enticed by offers of special powers. Making the agreement means their soul now belongs to the dark, and will remain so through future lifetimes. See Jessie's story in the chapter, Making Deals With The Devil, for an example of an attempt to create an agreement.

Extraterrestrials

Extraterrestrials are beings from other planets and other dimensions. Stories of their attachment to humans can be found in the chapter, The ET Story.

Healing Angels

These angels are called on to cleanse, heal and restore clients once the interference of an attached entity has been removed from them. The Healing Angels are also called to cleanse soul fragments before the fragments are returned to clients by the Rescue Angels.

Jesus

In Christian religions, Jesus is God come to earth to save mankind.

Light

In the context of this book, "light" refers to the form of pure energy that resides in all beings. See also "The Light" in this glossary.

Lost Souls

I have referred to all souls who are in need of assistance to cross the threshold into the Light—earthbound entities, dark force entities, displaced extraterrestrials—as lost souls. In addition, when dark force entities are restored to the Light, the earthbound entities they have captured, now free of the influence of the dark, are also in need of assistance to complete their journey to the Light. The Rescue Angels are called on to gather up the released souls and carry them to their place in the Light.

Portals

One of the ways dark force entities invade a victim is to establish an opening in the energy envelope that surrounds the human. Once this doorway, or portal, is made, dark force entities have free entry. A human so affected will have multiple attachments. See the chapters, Prisoners Of Darkness and Making Deals With The Devil, for examples of portals and how they are used.

Renunciation Of The Darkness

The declaration made to end an agreement made with the dark. The Renunciation of the Darkness can be found in Appendix 2.

Rescue Angels

Rescue Angels, working under the direction of Archangel Michael, carry lost souls to the Light. They also do the work of encapsulating dark force entities in light, and, later, escorting the dark force entities to their place in the Light.

Shamanism

Shamanism is a broadly used term referring to healers who practice soul traveling in a trance, or dreamlike state. Shamanism, as it applies to the work here, is discussed in the chapter, Soul Fragment Retrieval.

Soul Fragment Retrieval

A process of calling back parts of one's consciousness. In soul fragment retrieval, the Rescue Angels accompany the client in locating those fragmented pieces of the client's soul and return them to the client. See the chapter, Soul Fragment Retrieval, for more on this process.

Spirit Releasement

The process of helping hangers-on in the spirit world detach from their human hosts and find the way to their true homes. A more compassionate, usually less dramatic, and more effective form of exorcism.

The Dark

The dark is best described as "no light" rather than a substance in its own right. It seems to be dependent on the draining off of the lower energies produced by life forms capable of experiencing negative emotions in order to create a well of energy, as the ones who dwell in the darkness have lost sight of their own ability to draw in light.

The Light

The Light, our final destination after death, is referred to as Heaven in the Christian religions. Many earthbound entities, when they are reintroduced to the Light, refer to it as home.

In order to be freed from the influence of the dark, dark force entities who have newly discovered the light within them are asked to declare their allegiance to the Light. It has great significance to them to make this declaration. See also "Light" in this glossary.

Thoughtform

An aggregate of thoughts that forms a belief and seems to take on a life of its own. An example of a thoughtform is described in the chapter, Soul Fragment Retrieval.

Warrior Angels

Warrior Angels are called on to establish and hold a protective field of light at the beginning of a session to protect the client from the influence of dark force entities. Warrior Angels work under the direction of Archangel Michael.

Further Reading

Spirit Releasement

Instances of spirit attachment and spirit releasement therapy can be found in the following:

Baldwin, William J., Ph.D., *Spirit Releasement Therapy: A Technique Manual, Second Edition,* West Virginia, Headline Books, Inc. 1995. ISBN: 978-0-9299-1516-6

Baldwin, William J., Ph.D., *Healing Lost Souls: Releasing Unwanted Spirits from Your Energy Body,* Virginia, Hampton Roads Publishing Company, Inc. 2003. ISBN: 978-1-5717-4366-4

Baldwin, William J., Ph.D., *CE-VI: Close Encounters of the Possession Kind,* West Virginia, Headline Books, Inc. 1998. ISBN: 978-0-9299-1522-7

Fiore, Edith, Ph.D., *The Unquiet Dead: A Psychologist Treats Spirit Possession*, New York, Ballantine Books, Random House, Inc. 1995. ISBN: 978-0-3454-6087-5

Ireland-Frey, Louise, M.D., *Freeing the Captives: The Emerging Therapy of Treating Spirit Attachment,* Virginia, Hampton Roads Publishing Company, Inc. 1999. ISBN: 978-1-5717-4136-3.

Past Life Regression

Brian L. Weiss, M.D., brought attention to past life regression with the publication of his experiences with past life regression as therapy, now in print as the twentieth anniversary edition:
Weiss, Brian L., M.D., *Many Lives, Many Masters,* New York, Fireside, Simon & Shuster, Inc. 1988. ISBN: 978-0-6716-5786-4

Hypnotherapy

An introduction to hypnosis as therapy. Clearly laid out exercises offer an experience of the use of trance states in changing behavioral patterns:
Hadley, Josie and Carol Staudacher, *Hypnosis for Change, Third Edition,* California, New Harbinger Publications, Inc. 1996. ISBN: 978-1-5722-4057-5

For an entry into the complex and lyrical world of Milton Erickson's work, I refer you to:
Bandler, Richard and John Grinder, *Patterns of the Hypnotic Techniques of Milton H. Erickson, M.D., Volume 1,* California, Meta Publications, Inc. 1975. ISBN: 978-0-9169-9001-5

Awakening the Light Body

Sanaya Roman and Duane Packer, Ph.D., began teaching this form of meditation in 1989. It is now available in recorded form through LuminEssence Productions, P.O. Box 1310, Medford, OR 97501. The website is www.orindaben.com.

Index Of Stories

Made in the USA
San Bernardino, CA
08 January 2016